M000286643

# New Beginning
### I've accepted Christ - now what?

## A Discipleship Guide for New Believers

**JnJ Publishing**
Real, Practical and Super-natural; Ministry Resources for the
Next Generation
For Questions or Comments: www.JnJpublishing.com

ISBN 978-0615499116

JnJ Publishing
Columbia, Maryland, U.S.A.
Printed in the United States of America
2011 – First Edition

# Table of Contents

# Part 4: Spiritual Growth ........................................ 141

# Part 5: Knowing God's Will .................................. 169

# Appendix:

# Acknowledgments

Joseph: First and foremost, I want to acknowledge the mercy and grace of God who has allowed me a deeper, richer, and more intimate relationship with the Lord Jesus Christ. With the titanic task of completing this book while working as a full time minister and being a father and husband, I was strengthened when the Lord intervened to bring me many prayer warriors in order to help me complete this book. Thanks goes to my wife Jackie and my children Grace, Ashleigh, and Colin along with many others who have faithfully and frequently prayed for me so that I could complete this project. Without their prayers, I could not have finished this monumental undertaking.

Jae: Praise the Lord who has given me the opportunity to express my teaching gift through writing. Although I have always had the ambition to write, it wasn't until I met Joseph that the Lord combined the gift with the medium. I would like to thank my wife Sue Jean and children: Simeon, Hope, Jonah, Isaac, and Elijah who encouraged me to write my stories into a book. Well, here is the first...finally.

Our sincere gratitude goes to our cover designer Ann Pak who is a freelance photographer and public school teacher in Maryland. She is passionate about God's love and beauty in all things and shares her passion through a creative lens. She donated her time and talent to produce the beautiful cover you are holding in your hand. Please visit http://annyphotography.com to see her other masterpieces.

Finally, we would like to thank you for buying and reading this book. You are either a new Christian or reading as one. We are thrilled that you want to follow the Lord more closely. May the LORD bless you in your endeavor to grow to be more like Him.

# INTRODUCTION

I (Joseph) accepted Christ at age 17 when I took a friend's invitation to attend his church retreat. The retreat speaker communicated the important message of living a holy life and asked everyone to pray and seek God's invitation. Well, there was one problem. I didn't know who God was. I had attended church on Sundays, but I never knew God on a personal level, so to ask an Almighty God to lead me in living a holy life was something very awkward. The time came for prayer and everyone bowed their heads and started to pray while light Christian music was playing in the background. I never learned how to pray to a living God before, so I just closed my eyes. That night was the night that I would never forget. I truly wanted to live a different kind of life, and I longed for a personal God to be present in my heart.

I was born in Seoul, Korea as child number six and given the name Yong Jin Choi. My oldest brother's name is Yong Woon Choi, my second oldest brother is Yong Duk Choi and my third oldest brother is Yong Sung Choi. You can imagine friends, family members, and even my own parents and siblings getting our names mixed up every time they called us. I have two older sisters, the first sister being my oldest sibling and the second being the sister right above me. I believe my sister Susan (her American name) who is right above me, did call me by my correct name since I was closest to her in age. Every time my sister Susan would call me by my correct

1

name, I felt like I was truly a part of the family and had some identity in the home.

My father was hardly around, always somewhere else but never at home; so basically, my mother stepped up as a "single" parent selling fish in the market place along with real estate to provide the very basic necessities for the children. My older brothers and sisters would wear the same clothes for months and sometimes not eat for a few days, so that the younger ones could eat. Post Korean War was difficult for everyone, but my father was able to find a job. He worked, but used the money he earned on everything else except his family. Even after we came to America, he still lived his own life, so the family had to find ways to keep living and working with no "head" support. This is why my older siblings, especially my brothers, struggled to find their own identity within the family and in the new society, culture, and language.

I grew up never knowing my father, and when he died, I had many regrets. With unhealthy eating and smoking, he died in his early sixties. Since our father's presence and authority was absent, by the time we came to America, there was much difficulty among all my siblings. Children, especially boys, need the emotional along with the physical presence of their fathers to guide, direct, and protect them, and to give them wise counsel through life's situations, and without them boys will struggle to become men.

So, when I closed my eyes to pray, this was the emptiness that was running through my heart. I needed a solid male role model and a father who would guide and help me understand what it meant to become a man. At 17 at the Christian retreat center, I asked Jesus Christ to come into my heart and be the male role model that I was so desperately seeking. Tears started to roll down my cheeks and my heart was filled with peace and joy. I started to praise Him, thank Him, and felt as if I was the only person in the room. That unforgettable night was the day that I truly met God who transformed my heart to know Him as a personal God. Along with many other people I let my friends and pastors know that I accepted Christ, and they were thrilled. Many came and congratulated me; however, after the retreat, it seemed that everything went back to life as usual with some basic changes. I participated more in youth events and Sunday worship, but no one really guided me on what I was supposed to do next after I accepted Christ. I was basically told to just read the Word, pray, go to church on Sundays and continually seek God. The youth pastor did not have the one-on-one time to help me go through the basics of the Christian life. He was too busy trying to run the programs of his ministry. In general, most pastors are too busy to have one-on-one discipleship with their church members. So, they don't take the time to establish a new believer in Christian fundamentals. Church leaders and volunteers are in the same boat as the pastors, too busy to disciple.

Throughout my ministry experience, I realized it is very common for churches to plug people (believers and non-believers) into Sunday worship services hoping that those who just accepted Christ will progress toward spiritual maturity on their own. Sure, there are many being assimilated into small, life, or cell groups for accountability and encouraged to volunteer for church services, but realistically, many are not being grounded on the essentials of Christian living.

As a Christian I had opportunities to work with many wonderful people serving in local churches. Many new believers serve the church simply because the church leadership requests the congregation members to do so while others just attend without knowing what they are supposed to do as Christians. In fact, I was even witnessing and evangelizing to a woman who had been serving in her local church for many years. She did not believe that Jesus was truly God. Countless numbers of new believers only attend Sunday worship, not developing or growing in their Christian walk. So when tests and trials come their way, they are shaken in their faith. As a result, many new believers fall back into their old lifestyle and step back from attending church, while some fall into the hands of religious cults because they don't know how to distinguish truth from error. They are persuaded through false promises and hopes. Unless a person has grown up in a solid church before becoming a believer, he will lack the understanding of the essential principles and doctrines of the Christian faith. This lack of a foundation prevents him from being firmly established.

This book was written to bridge the gap, to help new believers to become more acquainted with the Christian faith in order that they may become fully devoted followers of Jesus Christ. When we accept Jesus Christ as Lord and Savior, we are given a new identity, a child of God. And maturing as a child of God will take time, energy, and investment. We pray that this book will help to establish new believers in the maturing process. May the Lord bless your *New Beginning*.

**Are you busy** and don't have much time to read a book? Don't worry. This book contains steps, key points, and explanations for those who are pressed for time and find it difficult to read the entire book in a reasonable amount of time. This way you can still apply the principles in it while reading the rest of the book at your leisure. Go through the book and just read the **"Short Answers"** for quick and practical steps in moving forward in your walk with the Lord. Hopefully, we will whet your appetite for a fuller reading after you have gotten a taste.

**Sample:**

---

**Short Answers**:  Finding the right church.

**Step 1**:

**Step 2**:

**Step 3**:

---

**Short Answers**:  Finding the right Bible translation.

**Option 1**:

**Option 2**:

**Option 3**:

---

## Isaiah 53

[1] Who has believed our message
and to whom has the arm of the LORD been revealed?
[2] He grew up before him like a tender shoot,
and like a root out of dry ground.
He had no beauty or majesty to attract us to him,
nothing in his appearance that we should desire him.
[3] He was despised and rejected by mankind,
a man of suffering, and familiar with pain.
Like one from whom people hide their faces
he was despised, and we held him in low esteem.
[4] Surely he took up our pain
and bore our suffering,
yet we considered him punished by God,
stricken by him, and afflicted.
[5] But he was pierced for our transgressions,
he was crushed for our iniquities;
the punishment that brought us peace was on him,
and by his wounds we are healed.
[6] We all, like sheep, have gone astray,
each of us has turned to our own way;
and the LORD has laid on him
the iniquity of us all.
[7] He was oppressed and afflicted,
yet he did not open his mouth;
he was led like a lamb to the slaughter,

and as a sheep before its shearers is silent,

so he did not open his mouth.

[8] By oppression and judgment he was taken away.

Yet who of his generation protested?

For he was cut off from the land of the living;

for the transgression of my people he was punished.

[9] He was assigned a grave with the wicked,

and with the rich in his death,

though he had done no violence,

nor was any deceit in his mouth.

[10] Yet it was the LORD's will to crush him and cause him to

suffer,

and though the LORD makes his life an offering for sin,

he will see his offspring and prolong his days,

and the will of the LORD will prosper in his hand.

[11] After he has suffered,

he will see the light of life and be satisfied;

by his knowledge my righteous servant will justify many,

and he will bear their iniquities.

[12] Therefore I will give him a portion among the great,

and he will divide the spoils with the strong,

because he poured out his life unto death,

and was numbered with the transgressors.

For he bore the sin of many,

and made intercession for the transgressors.

# Part 1

# The Bible

The very first thing you have to obtain as a new believer is a Bible. The Bible is the written message from God to mankind, revealing to men their purpose in life. The Holy Bible was not written as a historical record per se, but as a divine guide book for mankind to know how to have a relationship with Him.

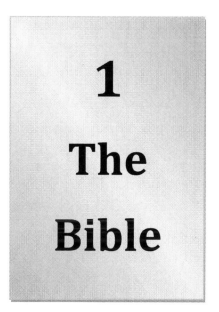

1

The

Bible

The 66 books of the Bible contain one theme even though 40 different authors with various backgrounds wrote it over a period of about 1,600 years. The Bible is divided into two parts. The first is called the Old Testament, containing 39 books of Hebrew Scriptures, and the second portion is called the New Testament, containing a set of 27 books. The first four books of the New Testament form the gospels which recount the life and ministry of Christ and are central to the Christian faith.

The writers came from all walks of life, including a king, a peasant, a philosopher, a fishermen, a herdsmen, a poet, a statesmen, a scholar, a soldier, a priest, a prophet, a tax collector, a rabbi, and a gentile doctor. The languages of the Bible or Holy Scriptures were Hebrew, Aramaic, and Greek. Throughout history mankind has not demonstrated unity in thought in any one area, yet the Holy Scriptures is perfect in unity among all the books. There is not a single composition throughout man's history that has ever been even close to such a miracle. This kind of coherent compilation can only be orchestrated by God, who was guiding all these writers. And, God has preserved His Word. In the spring of 1947, the Dead Sea Scrolls were discovered. These manuscripts were copies of large portions of the Old Testament (along with extra-biblical writings) a thousand years older than any other existing copies. The study of the scrolls has revealed that the Bible has not changed in content down through the generations.

**Short Answers**:  In order to find the right Bible, you need to find the right church.  Normally, churches will use one primary translation of the Bible, so finding the right church will be helpful in deciding the right type of Bible to own.

**Step 1**:  Know the essential doctrines of the Christian faith.  Knowing the essential doctrines will help you distinguish between truth and error when visiting churches. [Go to Part 2 "Essential Doctrines" for details]

**Step 2**: Drive around your community. [Go to chapter 2 "Finding the Right Church" for more details]

**Continuation**:

**Step 3**: Check out at least three churches through the church's website. Make sure to read their beliefs or "Statement of Faith".

**Step 4**: Go visit those that you have checked through the internet. Make sure to visit three or more.

**Step 5**: Interview or talk with the leadership team about what you are looking for in a church.

**Step 6**: Pray (If married, pray with your spouse). Not sure how to pray, read the section on prayer. See chapter 12.

**Step 7**: Purchase the Bible from a Christian book store, your home church, internet, or obtain it from Christian friends and family.

## Why is it Important to Read and Study the Bible?

It is vital to read and study the Bible in order to know what God desires from us as new creations in Christ. Before we accepted Jesus Christ as the Lord of our lives, Savior of our souls, and Master over our destinies, we only knew darkness and lived independently of the true source of life. 2 Corinthians 5:17 tell us that a "new creation has come: The old has gone, the new is here," and we must now follow the new path which is a totally different way of life than our old one. You must have a new outlook. Your new view must come from a biblical perspective, and you must now see through Jesus' eyes. As new believers, you must recognize that Jesus is the only "way and the truth and the life" through whom we can truly have peace and balance during our time here on earth before we go to heaven (John 14:6).

The only source of understanding "the way and the truth and the life" is the Word of God.

### 2 Timothy 3:16-17 (NIV)

[16] All Scripture is God-breathed and is useful for teaching, rebuking, correcting and training in righteousness, [17] so that the servant of God may be thoroughly equipped for every good work.

The Bible remains the only reliable source of divine revelation, sustaining you as a Christian in your walk with God. The following are significant promises from the Bible.

**The Bible is the source of:**

- Truth: "Sanctify them by the truth; your word is truth" (John 17:17).

- <u>God's blessing</u>: "He replied, 'blessed are those who hear the word of God and obey it'" (Luke 11:28).
- <u>Victory</u>: "...the sword of the Spirit, which is the word of God" (Eph. 6:17).
- <u>Growth</u>: "Like newborn babies, crave pure spiritual milk, so that by it you may grow up in your salvation" (1 Pet. 2:2).
- <u>Power</u>: "I am not ashamed of the gospel, because it is the power of God for the salvation of everyone who believes: first for the Jew, then for the Gentile" (Rom. 1:16).
- <u>Guidance</u>: "Your word is a lamp to my feet and a light for my path" (Ps. 119:105).

**The Bible is your counselor and supporter in times of trial and suffering:**

**God will deliver you**: [10]"He has delivered us from such a deadly peril, and he will deliver us again. On him we have set our hope that he will continue to deliver us, [11] as you help us by your prayers. Then many will give thanks on our behalf for the gracious favor granted us in answer to the prayers of many" (2 Cor. 1:10 – 11).

**Jesus Christ gives peace and rest**: [28]"Come to me, all you who are weary and burdened, and I will give you rest. [29] Take my yoke upon you and learn from me, for I am gentle and humble in heart, and you will find rest for your souls. [30] For my yoke is easy and my burden is light" (Matt. 11:28 – 30).

**Hope for the soul**: [19]"We have this hope as an anchor for the soul, firm and secure. It enters the inner sanctuary behind the curtain, [20] where our forerunner, Jesus, has entered on our behalf. He has become a high priest forever, in the order of Melchizedek" (Heb. 6: 19 – 20).

**God's protective care**: [5]"For in the day of trouble he will keep me safe in his dwelling; he will hide me in the shelter of his sacred tent and set me high upon a rock. [6]Then my head will be exalted above the enemies who surround me; at his sacred tent I will sacrifice with shouts of joy; I will sing and make music to the LORD" (Psalm 27:5 – 6).

**God answers all important questions in life through the Bible:**

Other world views and secular philosophers have not been able to answer questions that truly shed light on the discussion of human significance. They have run up against a wall when trying to answer them because they want to keep God out of the discussion. But God answers our deepest questions through His Holy Bible.

- Am I significant?
- What is God's will for my life?
- Do I have a special calling from God?

- Where did I come from?
- Is there life after death?
- How do I get to heaven?
- Why is the world full of evil?
- Why do I struggle to do good?
- Is there only one way to heaven?

In addition to these "big" questions, the Bible has practical advice for such questions as:

- How do I find the right person to marry?
- How can I have a successful marriage?
- How can I raise my children God's way?
- How can I do business with integrity?
- How does God see success, and how do I achieve it?
- What really matters in life?
- How can I live so that I do not look back with regret?
- How can I handle the unfair circumstances and bad events of life victoriously?
- How do I forgive someone who has hurt me deeply?
- How do I reconcile with others?
- How do I deal with my anxieties and worries?

In reading the Bible you realize that God does not change nor does the nature of man. The Bible is as relevant for us today as it was when it was written thousands of years ago. While culture, environment, governments, and technology change, the basic nature of man (good and evil) never changes. And while mankind as a whole continues to seek love and satisfaction in all the wrong places, God—our good and gracious Creator—gives us the truth about lasting joy and peace, while the world only brings short term satisfaction. God's revealed Word, the Bible, is so important to human vitality that this is what Jesus said of it, "Man does not live on bread alone, but by every word that comes from the mouth of God" (Matthew 4:4).

# -Chapter 1-

# Different Translations of the Bible

The Holy Scriptures were written in three different languages: Hebrew, Aramaic, and Greek, and there are two primary groups of interpretations for the Bible. One is known as the Dynamic equivalent translations which are those that translate "phrase by phrase" rather than word for word. The Formal translations attempt a word for word interpretation, providing as literal a translation as possible. Dynamic equivalency is like a paraphrase, trying to convey ideas thought by thought. The primary objective of this type of translation is to give the reader the main idea of the sentence.

Advocates of this method believe that such a translation is closer to the original, in that it provides the readers insight into what the author really intended his first readers to understand. Others, however, believe that this method is too ambiguous, preferring the more literal word for word method of the King James Version (KJV), New American Standard Bible (NASB) and American Standard Version (ASV). Paraphrases make no effort to translate; they attempt to restate the ideas in modern language. Many times, the differences are often significant between a paraphrase and a literal translation. However, sometimes a good paraphrase will surface a shade of meaning or will illustrate the significance of a clause or phrase better because they have thought through the nuances of the words used, and these insights can add value to the reader's understanding of the Bible. Some versions of the Bible are really between Dynamic and Formal; these include the New Revised Standard Version (NRSV) and the New Living Translation (NLT). The following is an example of the different variations.

New International Version (NIV): Hebrews 12:1-3

*Therefore, since we are surrounded by such a great cloud of witnesses, let us throw off everything that hinders and the sin that so easily entangles, and let us run with perseverance the race marked out for us. Let us fix our eyes on Jesus, the author and perfecter of our faith, who for the joy set before him endured the cross, scorning its shame, and sat down at the right hand of the throne of God. Consider him who endured such opposition from sinful men, so that you will not grow weary and lose heart.*

King James Version (KJV): Hebrews 12:1-3

*Wherefore seeing we also are compassed about with so great a cloud of witnesses, let us lay aside every weight, and the sin which doth so easily beset us, and let us run with patience the race that is set before us, looking unto Jesus the author and finisher of our faith; who for the joy that was set before him endured the cross, despising the shame, and is set down at the right hand of the throne of God. For consider him that endured such contradiction of sinners against himself, lest ye be wearied and faint in your minds.*

New American Standard Bible: Hebrews 12:1-3

*Therefore, since we have so great a cloud of witnesses surrounding us, let us also lay aside every encumbrance and the sin which so easily entangles us, and let us run with endurance the race that is set before us, fixing our eyes on Jesus, the author and perfecter of faith, who for the joy set before Him endured the cross, despising the shame, and has sat down at the right hand of the throne of God. For consider Him who has endured such hostility by sinners against Himself, so that you will not grow weary and lose heart.*

**Different Translation and Versions:**

New International Version (NIV)
New American Standard Bible (NASB)
The Message
Amplified Bible
New Living Translation (NLT)
King James Version (KJV)
English Standard Version (ESV)
Contemporary English Version (CEV)
New King James Version (NKJV)
American Standard Version (ASV)
With so many Bible translations to choose from, it's hard to know which one is right for you.

## Which Bible Version or Translation is Recommended?

**Short Answers**: Finding the Right Bible Translation for you.

**Option 1**: Best recommended Bible is the one written in Hebrew and Greek.

**Option 2**: If you do not know how to read it in Hebrew and Greek, then find the translation that is best understood by you or obtain one that is the most popular among Christians.

**Option 3**: Find a home church and find out which Bible translation is most used. Use the Bible recommended by your home church for reading and studying.

**Option 4**: Get one of each, a Dynamic and a Formal. If you have internet access, you don't have to buy a second Bible. Access every kind of Bible known to man at Biblegateway.com or Biblos.com or get an app for your smartphone.

You have to keep in mind that the Bible was originally written in Hebrew, Greek and Aramaic. Moses wrote the first five books by God's command and Exodus 34:27 records God's words to Moses saying, "Write down these words, for in accordance with these words I have made a covenant with you and with Israel." Moses wrote these words from his native language called Hebrew. Almost the entire Old Testament was written in Hebrew during the thousand years of its composition, but a few chapters in the prophecies of Ezra and Daniel were written in a language called Aramaic. Eventually Aramaic dominated the ancient world and became the common language spoken in Israel in Jesus' time. Some Aramaic words were even used by the Gospel writers in the New Testament. However, the New Testament was completed in Greek due to a new world order and the spread of the Greek culture and language. Over time, many Jews could not speak Hebrew and Aramaic, so around 300 BC a translation of the Old Testament from Hebrew into Greek was undertaken and was completed around 200 BC. Eventually, this Greek translation of the Old Testament, called the Septuagint, was widely accepted and was even used in many synagogues. The early Christians were able to use the new translations to spread the gospel throughout the world.

Please keep in mind that there is no one language that corresponds perfectly to any other language, and every translation involves some degree of interpretation. As a result these are the reasons for many different English versions or translations of the original writings of the Holy Scriptures in Hebrew, Aramaic, and Greek. How scholars view Scripture becomes extremely important in the final outcome of the Bible as they try to balance between readability and accuracy.

## Instead of Asking Which Bible Version or Translation Is Recommended, the Question Should Be Which Bible Translation Is Right for Me?

In order to find the right Bible, it would be best to find the right church first. Churches in general will use one particular type as the primary Scripture for use during worship service. So, it makes sense to find a home church before deciding on the translation since following the pastor in the translation he is using will make following his message easier. Therefore, choosing your home church should be a priority. Then it will be easier to choose the translation since more than likely the version will be chosen for you. But keep in mind that is not the only translation you can have. You can have as many translations as you can find or afford. With the internet most of them will be free. In any case the Holy Spirit will lead you into all truth as you strive to follow Him.

## Spiritual Leaders

The Bible is clear that we must be wise in our choice of "Spiritual Leaders" guiding us in our Christian journey. A leader causes others to follow some course of action, gives an ideology, or line of reasoning. Thus, a leader is one who influences followers to think or behave in a certain way. Accordingly, a spiritual leader is the one who leads others to seek out, understand, and live out the biblical principles and commands of the Bible. Therefore, finding a good Christian Bible teacher is important to our spiritual growth.

## 2 Peter 2:1 (NIV)

[1] But there were also false prophets among the people, just as there will be false teachers among you. They will secretly introduce destructive heresies, even denying the sovereign Lord who bought them—bringing swift destruction on themselves.

The Bible is unmistakable in its warning that there are false prophets among us, so finding the right church that declares and lives the truth is a matter of discernment. False teachers and false doctrine are a danger to the church. A false prophet, spiritual leader, or teacher may or may not know the truth but his teaching will be contrary to Scripture. For selfish gain he pursues people and tells them whatever they want to hear. There are many spiritual leaders today who prey upon those who are unaware of the truth.

## Matthew 7:15

Beware of false prophets, who come to you in sheep's clothing but inwardly are ravenous wolves.

Many cults have some truth in their doctrine which makes them even more dangerous to those who are untrained to discern truth from error. Jesus made it clear to all of us to "beware of false prophets, who come to you in sheep's clothing," and without understanding the truth of God's word, many will believe in lies. Even the famous New Testament writer, apostle Paul indicated, "I know that after I leave, savage wolves will come in among you and will not spare the flock" (Acts 20:29).

Consider the statement "God helps those who help themselves." Should we believe this? Is it biblical? If we held to this philosophy, then when we come across the passage, "I can do all things through *Him* who gives me strength" (Phil 4:13), we are confronted. Which one do we believe? Jesus also declares, "Apart from me you can do nothing" (John 15:5). Now we know that the statement is false according to Scripture. God wants us to follow Him and rely on His strength. He strengthens those who are His as it is written in 2 Chronicles 16:9: "For the eyes of the LORD range throughout the earth to strengthen those whose hearts are fully committed to him."

You will run into many such situations. Determine to believe God's word over everything else, including spiritual leaders. They can have the most devastating impact on your spiritual life. For more information about finding Christian mentors and Spiritual leaders go to chapter 14.

## Nehemiah 8:7-8

[7] The Levites—Jeshua, Bani, Sherebiah, Jamin, Akkub, Shabbethai, Hodiah, Maaseiah, Kelita, Azariah, Jozabad, Hanan and Pelaiah—instructed the people in the Law while the people were standing there. [8] They read from the Book of the Law of God, making it clear and giving the meaning so that the people understood what was being read.

## 1 Timothy 4:12-13

[12]Let no one despise you for your youth, but set the believers an example in speech, in conduct, in love, in faith, in purity. [13]Until I come, devote yourself to the public reading of Scripture, to exhortation, to teaching.

# -Chapter 2-

## Finding the Right Church

Finding the right church is a very significant move much like finding the right house. Home buyers do not move into the first house they see. They shop around. Looking at different houses takes time, energy and investment for the whole family. A significant time given brings "significance" to the home found.

The reality is there are no perfect churches. What makes a church in the first place is a group of sinners and "all have sinned and fall short of the glory of God," (Ro. 3:23, ESV). So finding a perfect place where everyone is a black belt in spiritual maturity will only be in heaven. In the mean-time we can consider some other options.

Before searching for a "spiritual home" consider how you and your family can serve in a church. Just attending church without any involvement can lead to a sense of estrangement. God created man in His image and placed in his heart the need to have a relationship with Him. He also made him social so mankind needs fellowship with one another. All married couples understand the importance of cultivating their relationship, and the marriage is built up when each decides to participate and serve the other. Therefore, considering how you can be part of your home church will be important to the success of your spiritual growth.

**Short Answers**: Finding the Right Church.

**Step 1**: Know the essential doctrines of the Christian Faith. Knowing the essential doctrines will help you distinguish between truth and error when visiting churches. [Go to Part 2 "Essential Doctrines" for details]

**Step 2**: Drive around your community.

**Step 3**: Check out at least three churches through the church website. Make sure to read their beliefs or "Statement of Faith."

**Step 4**: Go visit those that you have checked through the internet. Make sure to visit three or more.

**Step 5**: Interview or talk with the leadership team about what you are looking for in a church.

**Step 6**: Pray (If married, pray with your spouse).

- Not sure how to pray, read the section on prayer, Part 3, for "Short Answers" and details.

**Note**: If you were given the gospel message by a friend or family member, then visit their church.

## Know the Essential Doctrines of the Christian Faith

A section of this book is dedicated to "Essential Doctrines" that every believer must know to be established in the Christian faith. It is critical that new believers in Jesus Christ know and hold to these fundamental Christian beliefs because when anyone teaches false doctrine, it can be recognized and rejected.

In an analogy we can consider the "Essential Doctrines" to the basic components, functions, and structure of a car. There are literally hundreds of different models, styles, and makes of vehicles to choose from, and it can be very confusing for new car shoppers to determine which would be the right fit. However, it will be easier to spot a lemon if we knew what we were looking for. I wouldn't buy a sports car if I need a minivan that seats 8, but I have to be able to recognize the difference between a minivan and a sports car.

I (Joseph) remember going to a used car dealer and test running a vehicle to purchase. In the middle of the test drive, the engine started to fume black smoke. I told the sales guy that we should pull over because the smoke seemed to be getting worse. He told me not to worry because it was just a minor problem and they should be able to fix it in no time. I kept insisting that we should pull over and he just kept insisting that I continue to drive. I decided to take my life into my own hands, rejected the salesman's opinion, and pulled over. And sure enough as soon as we opened the hood, the engine caught on fire. The salesman quickly grabbed a fire extinguisher from his trunk and drowned the engine. I wonder why the extinguisher was in the car in the first place. The salesman told me that he'd give me a large discount. LoL. My incredulous look could have melted the polar icecap. Days later, I wondered if during the test drive had the engine not exposed the issue and I purchased it, what would have happened several months down the line. I could imagine the heartache of having to deal with a burning engine on our way to vacation. I would have put my life and the lives of my family in jeopardy. Because of this incident, I made sure I knew what a good engine was and what it was supposed to sound like. Although I was not a mechanic, I interviewed several mechanics and studied the basics of car functions so I would be able to make fundamental distinctions in engine characteristics. Even then I took the car to a professional mechanic for his opinion before I purchased the car.

In essence, the new believer in Jesus Christ must know the sound doctrines of the Christian faith, so that no spiritual-used-car salesman can sway you to purchase false doctrine. Without knowing the basics of the Christian faith, new believers will fall victim to "false prophets" and "false teachers" and end up in the spiritual highway with their cars in flames. Not only will your soul be in danger, but everyone else's you bring along.

**2 Peter 2:1-3**

[1] But there were also false prophets among the people, just as there will be false teachers among you. They will secretly introduce destructive heresies, even denying the sovereign Lord who bought them—bringing swift destruction on themselves. [2] Many will follow their depraved conduct and will bring the way of truth into disrepute. [3] In their greed these teachers will exploit you with fabricated stories. Their condemnation has long been hanging over them, and their destruction has not been sleeping.

## Drive Around Your Community or Search the Internet

Unless you live in a rural area, you will have a number of churches in your community. In some locations across the United States, there seems to be a church in every block. Since there are so many available, you must choose wisely. Pick at least three churches to investigate. As you search the church's website, thoroughly read the information about their "statement of faith" or "beliefs" or "core beliefs." Most evangelical churches will have similar beliefs, so the distinctions will occur in the church vision, mission, and core values. This is how you will know where the church is headed and whether you want to join them. The church programs and ministries just tell you what they do, not where they are headed. Analyzing their core values will reveal why they're doing it.

What does the Bible say about serving? Through service the body of believers will glorify God, build up and encourage one other, and reach unbelievers. Christians are directed by God to serve. The Bible tells us that "Each of you should use whatever gift you have received to serve others, as faithful stewards of God's grace in its various forms" (1 Peter 4:10), and this is one of the ways we worship God (1 Peter 4:11, Romans 12:1). When we do our part in using our God-given gifts to serve others, we are helping to build up the local church and the universal church-made up of all believers throughout the world: "... to equip his people for works of service, so that the body of Christ may be built up..." (Eph. 4:12).

In most cases those who have accepted Christ were influenced through a relationship of a friend or family member. If this is your case also, show them your gratitude by attending their church at first. You are not obligated to stay and later on may choose another, but know that your friends have demonstrated faithfulness to the Lord and a mindset that is positive enough to emulate. Their church must have done something right to have won you over. Find out what it is.

## Interview or Talk with the Leadership Team about What You are Looking for in a Church

In Matthew 7:24-27 Jesus said that the wise person always builds his house upon a rock, and the foolish person builds his house upon sand. What are some important questions to ask to find out about a church's underpinnings?

1. **The Church's View of Scripture:** Most evangelical protestant churches will not have drastic differences in the "Essential Doctrines" of the Christian faith; however, some denominations and churches will have a skewed view of the Holy Bible. You may not find out about this difference until you get heavily involved in the church, so do your research before you decide to join. Questions to ask: a) Does your church hold to the inspiration and inerrancy of the Scriptures? In other words, "Does your church believe that there are mistakes in the Bible?" b) Does your church believe the Bible is the only rule for faith and practice (2 Tim. 3:16; 2 Pet. 1:20–21)? c) Does your church offer Bible study classes or at least offer some way for people to study and learn about the Bible, besides Sundays? [Good churches will always offer or at least acknowledge the importance of studying the Word of God.] It is important for believers to be fed from the Word based upon Acts 20:27; 1 Tim. 4:13-16; and 2 Tim. 4:1-5. There should be a commitment from the church to teach the Word of God to those who desire it. As a matter of principle, the leadership should be initiating in this area.

34

2. **Prayer:** If no information is given either in the brochure of the church or on the internet, make it a point
   to ask if the church asks for prayer requests or offers
   prayer meetings. Some churches will even offer the opportunity for those needing prayer to make their requests through the internet. Bridgeway Community
   Church in Columbia, Maryland, for example, offers the
   option to ask for prayer via the web. On Tuesday nights
   members meet to pray over those requests, and after
   each worship service members pray for individuals
   who seek prayer. Remember, since you are looking for
   a church that prays, make sure you first pray for the
   guidance of the Holy Spirit in finding the right church.
   [For further understanding of prayer and how to pray,
   go to Part 3.]

3. **Programs and Outreach:** If not indicated by the church
   brochure or on their website, ask questions pertaining
   to the specific needs of the family. For example, get as
   much information on Youth or Teen programs if you
   have a youth in your household who will be attending
   the church with you. You may be interested in other
   areas such as Children's programs, Praise ministry,
   Men's and Women's ministry, Singles' ministry, College ministry and so forth. The church should also be
   doing "Outreach" programs such as feeding or sup-

porting the homeless and elderly, social justice ministry, prison ministry, aid to third world countries, to name a few.

## God's Love through His People

If you have ever gone house shopping, you know what it's like to walk into a home. Almost immediately, there is an emotional response that surfaces. The first impression may be based on knowledge, but they are emotional. Aaah! I like the place. I really like the place. I love the place. You can tell if the house feels like the home that you want. Is the house cold and gloomy or warm and inviting? This type of emotional response occurs when we walk into a church building. But unlike house shopping you are not evaluating a building. You are sensing the spirit of the people. Are they cold and gloomy or warm and inviting? Do they genuinely show joy or do they look like they're faking it? Are people mostly self-absorbed or are they seeking to minister to one another? Listen to the conversations around you. What are they talking about? Are they encouraging one another, or are they talking about trivial matters? Are the words critical or uplifting? Don't get distracted by your evaluation of the building; observe the people. They should show indications that they love one another as Christ commanded in John 13:34-35.

Remember that no church will be perfect. But they should display a balance of characteristics that define a good church. Is the Word of God central and honored? Is the sermon centered on the Bible or is the Bible only used as a proof text. Is Bible study emphasized as a theme of the church? Are they concerned about missions? Is evangelism the norm of the church? Is fellowship a regular part of the church program? Is the church growing both numerically and spiritually? Is the numerical growth by conversion or by transfer? In other words is the church growing because Christians are coming from other churches or are people getting converted through their ministry? All of these are healthy characteristics of a worthy church, and they should have them in proper balance, not overemphasizing some or de-emphasizing others. A balanced ministry is a Spirit-controlled ministry. If you find a church that possesses most but not all of the characteristics we've mentioned, don't immediately disregard it. Consider whether God wants to use you to help improve that local body as you exercise your own particular spiritual gifts. This is why it is important to pray before attending each of the various churches. Choosing a home church is one of the most significant decisions you will make--one that reaches into eternity. Spend as much time and effort in choosing a church as you would in purchasing a house.

# Why Should I Attend Church in the First Place?

In the Old Testament, the Israelites gathered in the temple to worship God, and families came together in homes to hear the powerful historical accounts that helped shape who they were. The New Testament frequently emphasizes the importance of gathering together as the body of believers. The author of Hebrews stresses the importance of the assembly:

### Hebrews 10:24-25

[24] And let us consider how we may spur one another on toward love and good deeds, [25] not giving up meeting together, as some are in the habit of doing, but encouraging one another—and all the more as you see the Day approaching.

It is only in the local body that a believer can experience a level of intimacy that makes fellowship and accountability possible. Although fellowship is discussed in chapter 15, a brief mention is necessary here because it is related to the mandate of belonging to a local body. Being around other Christians fills the emotional-needs tank. All humans are born with the need to connect relationally. If there isn't that connection to other human beings, we will dry up. Believers are especially in need of fellowship with other believers because we face so many oppositions. Satan, the world, and our sinful nature are fighting against us, so where will we get our strength to battle against them? Only with other Christians will we find the encouragement and kindred spirit to keep fighting instead of giving up.

Accountability is the same way. Only in the context of relationships is accountability possible. If I'm not committed to a local body, how will correction work? If someone tells me that I need to stop sinning, I could just leave and not hear about it anymore. Nothing in my life will ever get fully addressed. I can keep avoiding the issues of my life by migrating. Besides no one will be comfortable enough to exhort you and rebuke you if you don't belong to their body. I won't feel comfortable correcting a transient church member and he won't feel right getting correction from some church member he doesn't know well.

### Acts 2:42
They devoted themselves to the apostles' teaching and to fellowship, to the breaking of bread and to prayer.

And it is only in this setting that we can encourage one another. The New Testament also teaches that every believer is to be under the protection and nurture of the leadership of the local church. These godly men can shepherd the believer by encouraging, admonishing, and teaching him to live a righteous life. God provides accountability to us through them. Mature Christian leaders are our models of the way we should live.

"Remember your leaders, who spoke the word of God to you. Consider the outcome of their way of life and imitate their faith" (Hebrews 13:7).

Furthermore, in the New Testament, when Paul gave Timothy special instructions about the gathering of believers, he emphasized the importance of the public reading of the Holy Scriptures, exhortation, and teaching.

## 1 Timothy 4:13

Until I come, devote yourself to the public reading of Scripture, to preaching and to teaching.

The important part of the emphasis of public adoration or reading of God's holy Word includes the essential practice of hearing the Word (understanding God's heart), being called to obedience through exhortation (transformation of the heart), and teaching (knowledge of God). It is only in the context of the local assembly that these things can most effectively take place. God has ordained that the church provide the kind of environment where an uncompromising life can thrive.

# -Chapter 3-

## How to Read the Bible

### Once You Find the Right Church and the Right Bible, Then, How Do You Read the Bible?

Reading the Bible can be an intimidating task for a new believer. Many Christians, with good intentions to read God's Word, will have no real method of reading through it. In Christian book stores, there are many Bible study materials and other ministry resources to help new believers get acquainted with learning and growing in the Word of God. With so many varieties of learning materials and an already hectic life, new believers can be overwhelmed.

**Acts 17:11**

Now the Berean Jews were of more noble character than those in Thessalonica, for they received the message with great eagerness and examined the Scriptures every day to see if what Paul said was true.

The Bible reveals God, Christ, man, the past, and the future, but above all the Bible conveys the very life and heart of God. When we open ourselves to its message, it will liven up, refresh, strengthen, and transform our inward being. We must know the Bible. It is our life.

### Matthew 4:4

Man does not live by bread alone, but on every word that comes from the mouth of God.

**Short Answers**: How to Read the Bible.

**Step 1**: Give a one year commitment to God to read His Word. Go to Appendix B for the commitment form.

**Step 2**: Find a quiet place.

**Step 3**: Start from the Gospels in New Testament (Matthew, Mark, Luke, John). Get to know Jesus.

**Step 4**: Read a chapter at regular speed, slow speed, and regular speed again, then spend a few minutes meditating on what you just read.

**Step 5**: Write in your journal thoughts and questions from your reading (Strongly recommended).

**Step 6**: Memorize one verse a week, a verse that spoke to you.

## Give a One Year Commitment to Christ to Read the Bible

Do you want to know the secret to spiritual growth when reading the Bible? It is commitment. One night, I (Joseph) couldn't sleep, so I got up to watch some television. Since I didn't have cable, all the networks were showing infomercials (paid advertisement that runs as a program to sell a product), and they were all on losing weight. Each weight loss program continued every 30 minutes. I couldn't believe it, that all four networks were showing programs on losing weight at the same time. I got irritated at first, but then started to recognize a similar pattern with all the programs. I decided to write down the testimonies of all the people who lost weight and assured the audience that the product they used was guaranteed to work for anyone. The first weight loss program used natural supplements, the second used unique and special exercise routines, third used an exercise equipment, and the last used a series of psychological CDs guaranteed to help any person who listened to it, lose the weight.

As I wrote down the testimonies from each of the shows, the word "commitment" kept coming up. I asked myself, "How can the average person who watches all the weight loss programs know which one is best for him? Everybody is making the guarantee, so which one works the best?" What was interesting was that they all worked, but it was not the product or the exercise routine, but the individual who made the "commitment" that made it possible. Each of the weight loss winners stated they made up their mind to stick to the program for a certain length of time and follow the instructions to the letter. With the right attitude and commitment to stick to the plan, each of the participants using any method was able to lose the weight.

In reading the Bible it is imperative to have the right attitude and to make the commitment. I would encourage you to make a one year pledge to read a chapter a day and set a time either in the morning, noon, or evening for a duration of 15 minutes to an hour. You will increase your faith just by reading the Bible as it says in Romans 10:17 that "faith comes from hearing the message, and the message is heard through the word about Christ." Begin by signing a contract below which will help you start reading the Bible. People fail in their commitments to keep their new year's resolution because they don't feed their commitments, they don't have their commitments in writing, and they don't share their commitments with others. Get together with others who are reading their Bible so you can encourage one another, put your commitment in writing, and reward yourself monthly for completing it. Use the following commitment sheet as a tool and tape it to your mirror or computer or use it as the background of your Smart phone or as a screensaver of your computer. This will be a daily reminder of your commitment. If you miss a day, don't beat yourself up or quit. You are formulating a habit that should last a lifetime. Be patient but committed.

---

## Commitment

I (Print Name) _____ will make

a _____ (length of term) commitment to read the

Bible each day from day_____ to day_____

I pledge to give (Time length: 15 minutes to one hour) _____

in the (day or evening) _____ starting from

(month) _____ day _____ year _____

Sign Name: _____

Date: _____

Witness Name: _____

Date: _____

---

(Cutout on appendix B)

# Find a Quiet Place to Read the Bible

Every morning my alarm wakes me up for prayer and the reading of God's Word. I tried praying and reading the Bible in bed, but I consistently fell back to sleep; but I found what worked best for me was to go into my study and turn the lights on, away from anything that reminds me of more sleep.

It was during these quiet times in reading the Bible that I got to know the Lord on a more personal level. Read the Bible in a quiet place relatively free from distractions. Some people will read the Bible on a couch late at night when everyone else is asleep. Others will get up very early in the morning to read their Bible, and others find a quiet place at lunch time. A friend of mine has a large walk-in closet which he uses for prayer and the study of the Word. The primary objective is to be consistent with it. Like watering a plant, it is best to be regular and in set amounts for the greatest benefit. You are watering your soul and cultivating a relationship with your Savior.

## What Part of the Bible Do You Start Reading First?

Begin by developing a plan of how you will approach reading through the Bible. The best place to start is with the Gospels, which are the books of Matthew, Mark, Luke and John. These books document the life of Jesus and help us to believe in Him. They are at the beginning of the section called the New Testament. This is about three quarters of the way into your Bible. Your Bible has a table of contents in the front so you can look up the various books in the New Testament section. Remember, it is important to realize that the Bible is not an ordinary book that reads smoothly from cover to cover. It is actually a library, or collection of books written by different authors in several languages over 1600 years. Reading the Gospels (Matthew, Mark, Luke, and John) will familiarize you with Christ's life and ministry.

When reading the Bible, I would encourage you to read a chapter at regular speed, slow speed, and again at regular speed. Then spend a few minutes meditating on what you just read (RSR principle). Have you ever read something and asked yourself, "What did I just read?" Many of us throughout our academic studies have been in situations where we read a chapter and tried to figure out what we just read. The RSR principle which stands for R: Regular speed, S: Slow speed, and R: Regular speed will help you digest the words that are directly from God to you. Think of this analogy. The day before your mother passes away, she decides to write a letter to you, and few days later, the letter arrives at your house. How will you read the last words of your mother? I would assume, you would not read it like you would a newspaper or magazine. This letter from your mother would be so precious and valuable you would cherish every word in your heart. Thus, you must read the Bible with the same attitude.

It is important for Christians to meditate upon the Word of God and this does not involve maintaining a blank mind. Rather, it means filling the mind with the Word of God. In order for the Holy Spirit to effectively open your eyes, strengthen your faith, and affect your heart and mind, you must prayerfully focus your undivided attention upon the words you are reading. Meditating upon God's Word means thinking about what He is saying so that you can take His counsel and apply it to your daily life. As a result our hearts will be transformed, and we will become more like Christ. The purpose of meditation is to gain insight and understanding as you obey, so you'll care about the things you are obeying.

### Joshua 1:8

[8] Keep this Book of the Law always on your lips; meditate on it day and night, so that you may be careful to do everything written in it. Then you will be prosperous and successful.

## Why Should I Journal?

As I started to read the Bible on a daily basis, many questions came to mind concerning the chapter I just read. I started to write them in a notebook. Below are some questions that are strongly recommended by scholars to ask yourself when reading the Bible:

1. What is the passage saying to me?
2. What is it saying about God, Jesus, or the Holy Spirit?
3. Is there a command for me to obey?
4. What principle is this chapter teaching me?
5. Is this teaching me something right now?
6. What particular verse is speaking to me?

7. How can I apply this principle, command, warning and or teaching in my life?

Or simply ask: What does this mean?

This is why it is important to have a pen and notebook when you study God's Word. Jot down the questions that come up and try to answer them. Majority of the time the Bible itself will answer the questions you have. If you cannot find the answers, then it is best to seek your pastor or another teacher to find the answers. You may also consult a Bible commentary, but even if you do find your answer in a commentary, talk to your pastor about what you learned or read. In Acts 8:30, Philip asked the Ethiopian eunuch, "Do you understand what you are reading?" Or put it another way, "What does the Bible mean by what it says?" It is not enough to read the text and jump directly into application--you must first determine what it means, otherwise you may misapply the text.

Jesus made this promise to those who carry their personal Bible study through to this point: "If you know these things, blessed are you if you do them" (John 13:17). Having read and interpreted the Bible, you now have a basic understanding of what the Bible says, and what it means by what it says. But studying the Bible does not stop there. The ultimate goal is to let it speak to you in order to be more like God Himself. That requires personal application. If there is a command to be obeyed, obey it. If there is a promise to be embraced, claim it. If there is a warning to be followed, heed it. This is the ultimate step: submit to Scripture and let it transform your life.

The last stage of Bible study connects the doctrine you have learned in a particular passage with divine truths and principles taught elsewhere in the Bible to form the big picture. This process is called correlation. Always keep in mind that the Bible is one book in sixty-six parts, and it contains a number of truths and principles, taught over and over in a variety of ways and situations. By correlating and cross-referencing, you will begin to build a sound doctrinal foundation on which to live the Christian life.

### 1 Peter 2:2
Like newborn babies, crave pure spiritual milk, so that by it you may grow up in your salvation.

# Part 2

# Essential Doctrines

T he culture and the generation that we live in today make it difficult for believers to live out their faith, especially new Christians. Satan works hard to bring down believers with strong temptations, and religious cults make reasonable and logical

# 2

# Essential Doctrines

sounding statements to deter new believers from their faith. Two Mormons approached me when I was a young believer. They started asking me questions about the Bible, and with limited knowledge I (Joseph) felt I answered their questions adequately, but they brought up much deeper issues that really tested my belief in the Bible and Jesus. In my heart, I knew something was not right, but I didn't know exactly what it was until I did some research on what they believed. To them Jesus wasn't God nor was He the way of salvation. But in John 14:6 Jesus tells us "I am the way and the truth and the life. No one comes to the Father except through me." The approach by the Mormons to test my faith was just the beginning. Men and women from cults (religions that don't believe Jesus is God) such as Jehovah Witnesses, Buddhists, Hindus,

Christian Scientists, Moonies, and much more have approached me to either challenge my faith or test my knowledge of the Scriptures. Christianity in general has been attacked by atheists, cults, the government, and just about anyone who hates the name of Jesus, and Christians are vulnerable if they are unable to defend their faith due to their lack of knowledge of the foundational doctrines. Satan will by any means expose this weakness in order to shipwreck the believer's faith.

When I (Jae) became a Christian, my family was the first to attack my faith. Our family friend also accused me of being brainwashed and concluded that at best I was going through a phase. The floor-mates in my dorm told me that I shouldn't believe in fables as intelligent as I was. So with all the negative feedback I was receiving, I was completely disillusioned and wanted to give up. I told God that I resolved to know nothing accept that He is God, Jesus is His Son and the Savior of the world, and anyone can have an eternal relationship with Him by exercising faith in His death and resurrection to take away sin. Apart from that I told Him that He would have to build on it because I wasn't about to lose my mind regarding the details of theology.

1 Peter 5:8 reminds believers to "Be sober-minded; be watchful. Your adversary the devil prowls around like a roaring lion, seeking someone to devour." In order for you to stand strong and be rooted in your faith, you must understand

the essentials of the Christian faith. 1 Peter 3:15 says, "but in your hearts honor Christ the Lord as holy, always being prepared to make a defense to anyone who asks you for a reason for the hope that is in you; yet do it with gentleness and respect." This verse says three important things. The first is the command that "we" (all who accepted Jesus Christ as Lord) should be *ready* to answer questions about our faith in Jesus Christ. Second, we are to give a reason for the faith we have. Finally, If Jesus is truly Lord of our lives, then we should be obedient to Him by applying what the Bible says as in 2 Cor. 10:5, "We destroy arguments and every lofty opinion raised against the knowledge of God, and take every thought captive to obey Christ."

One of the primary reasons why Christians today need to know the essential doctrines (systems of beliefs) of our faith is because there are many false religions and counterfeit forms of Christianity. Without the knowledge of the truth, any cult, skeptic, or deceiver can lead you astray. A solid relationship with the Lord begins with the correct understanding of who God is and what Christianity is about. The central doctrines are the core beliefs that hold the Christian faith together. Without them the faith wouldn't be called Christianity.

**Short Answers**: Basic Doctrines of Christian Faith

**Step 1**: Know Scripture verses that confirm your faith: Go to chapter 9 "Confirm Your Faith," for more details.

**Step 2**: (Short Explanation of each doctrine)

- Atoning work of Christ on the cross: God forgives man's sins through the sacrifice of Jesus Christ on the cross.

- Resurrection of Jesus: 1 Corinthians 15:14-20

14 And if Christ has not been raised, our preaching is useless and so is your faith. 15 More than that, we are then found to be false witnesses about God, for we have testified about God that he raised Christ from the dead. But he did not raise him if in fact the dead are not raised. 16 For if the dead are not raised, then Christ has not been raised either. 17 And if Christ has not been raised, your faith is futile; you are still in your sins. 18 Then those also who have fallen asleep in Christ are lost. 19 If only for this life we have hope in Christ, we are of all people most to be pitied. 20 But Christ has indeed been raised from the dead, the first fruits of those who have fallen asleep.

**Continuation**:

- Deity of Jesus Christ:
  "while we wait for the blessed hope—the appearing of the glory of our great God and Savior, Jesus Christ," (Titus 2:13) and "Salvation is found in no one else, for there is no other name under heaven given to mankind by which we must be saved" (Acts 4:12).

- Trinity: 1 John 5:7 says, "For there are three that testify." (also Matt 28:20)

  o God is one. (Deu 6:4-5)
  o The Father is God (Isa 43:10-11) (Isa 44:6)
  o Jesus is God (John 1:1) (John 10:30) (Col 2:9)
  o The Holy Spirit is God (Act 5:3-4)
  o God is one (Exodus 20:2-3)
  o One God in three persons. The Trinity.

- Salvation by grace through faith: "For it is by grace you have been saved, through faith—and this is not from yourselves, it is the gift of God" (Ephesians 2:8).

Certain Christian doctrines constitute the core of the faith. Central doctrines include:

- Atoning work of Christ on the cross
- Bodily resurrection of Jesus
- Deity of Jesus Christ
- Trinity
- Salvation by Grace through Faith.

These essential beliefs encompass the essence of the Christian faith. The Scriptures teach that the beliefs mentioned above are of central importance because they define Christianity, and one cannot be saved and deny any of them.

## DOCTRINE of the Godhead

**Trinity:**
When talking about the attributes (unchanging and unique nature) of God, no words will be sufficient or comprehensive in its definition. All words will fall short of the true nature of God's unchanging, transcendent (outside of time and space), and immutable (impossible to destroy) characteristics. Biblically speaking God is **"Light"** (1 John 1:5), God is **"Spirit"** (John 4:24), and God is **"Love"** (1 John 4:8). He can be described in all three ways, but it is still not good enough. The word "trinity" does not exist in the Bible, even though we re-

fer to Him in that way. God is one God existing in three "persons" (for a lack of a better word) as the Father, the Son, and the Holy Spirit.

## God the Father:

God the Father is the first person of the trinity over everything, self-existing, and creator of all that exists. To Him we must give an account because He is the final authority and He alone deserves and demands our total loyalty. Even though He is invisible, he reveals Himself in light. (Genesis 1:26; Deuteronomy 6:4; John 1:18; 1 Corinthians 11:3; Eph 4:6)

## God the Son, Jesus Christ:

Jesus is the Son of God, the second person of the trinity, being made flesh from the Word of God, submitting to the Father but equal to Him and deserving equal worship. Jesus was conceived by the Holy Spirit in the Virgin Mary and was born into the world. Jesus is the only sufficient sacrifice for humanity's sins and who alone can reveal the true character of God. He was the only sinless God-man worthy enough to be worshipped. When we talk about Jesus as man or as God, we must understand that when He became man, He never ceased to be fully God. All of His deity was embedded in the human body that He inherited. He is all God and all man at the same time (Matthew 1:21; Luke 1:35; John 1:14; Hebrews 1:8; Col 2:9). Jesus was raised from the dead bodily and ascended into heaven where he sits at God's right hand waiting to judge the world at the end of all things. Jesus' death on the cross is complete payment for the sins of anyone who will trust in Him (2 Corinthians 5:21; Hebrews 9:22; Colossians 1:20-22, Romans 1:4; 1 Corinthians 15:3-4, 14-17; Ephesians 4:7-10; 1 Timothy 2:5).

**God the Holy Spirit:**

The Holy Spirit is the third person of the trinity whose work is to give man spiritual rebirth and be his helper by being the non-physical presence of Jesus on earth indwelling every believer. He brings illumination to the Scriptures, enables us to resist temptation, prompts us to practice righteousness, and intercedes for us in prayer. The Holy Spirit will remind us of the words of Jesus, convict us of sin, and guide us into all truth (John 15:26, 16:8-11; Acts 1:8; Romans 8:9; 1 Corinthians 2:10-12, 12:13; 2 Corinthians 3:18; Ephesians 1:13).

**Sin:**

The simple definition of sin is anything that is contrary to the character of God. "Be holy because I am holy," is what He said. Anything outside of that is sin. Whether it is a sin of commission or omission, if it is outside of the character of God, we have sinned. In other words if we do something we shouldn't or not do something we should have, we have violated the character of God and therefore sinned. Sin includes disobedience, actions without faith, and actions devoid of love (Lev 26:3-4; James 4:17; 1 Pet 1:16; Rom 14:23; 1 Cor 8:11-13). Be careful though that you don't get caught up in trying to avoid prohibitions. We will rarely sin if we are too busy doing what is good.

## Man:

Mankind is created in the image of God with free will for intimate fellowship with Him. However, man is utterly depraved and sinful from birth as the result of Adam's sin, unable to please God and destined for destruction. Man is therefore in need of forgiveness in order to avoid eternal separation from God. But God loves mankind and is unwilling that any be sent to eternal destruction. He must turn his life over to the Lord so that He can transform him into the image of Jesus. Only if mankind is willing, will God do the work (Genesis 1:26; Romans 3:9, 23, 5:12; Psalms 51:5; John 3:16; 1 Timothy 2:3, 2 Peter 3:9).

## Salvation:

Mankind is given the opportunity to experience forgiveness of their sins through the death and resurrection of Jesus Christ. Anyone who puts his trust in Christ's sacrifice for mankind receives forgiveness of sins and will never be separated from God even after death. Jesus alone is the mediator between

God and man, and salvation is found in no other. This salvation is by grace through faith, a gift which no one can earn. Salvation cannot be achieved through works; it must be received by faith (John 1:12, 3:5-7, 16; 10:28-29; 14:6; 1 John 5:11-12; Acts 4:12, Romans 3:24; 8:37-39; Galatians 2:16,21; Ephesians 2:1, 8, 9, 1 Timothy 2:5, Titus 3:5 , 1 Pet 3:18).

**The Church:**

The church is not a building but the people of God who trusted in Christ and is called to perpetuate the good news of forgiveness. Those who belong to Christ are to live out the principles of the Word of God while calling others to do the same. As God's children we are brothers and sisters who reflect His image and represent Him on earth (Matthew 28:18-20; Acts 2:41, 3:36-38; 1 Corinthians 11:25-26, 12:13; Ephesians 1:22-23; Philippians 1:1; Romans 8:29).

# -Chapter 4-

## Doctrine of the Atonement

The traditional definition of atonement is the reconciliation of God and man through the suffering and death of Jesus. The words amends, reparation, expiation are used to describe the process of correcting for wrongs committed. In Christianity atonement is achieved by appeasing divine anger caused by humanity's sin or by expiating or making satisfaction for the offense that caused the broken relationship.

### Leviticus 17:11

[11] For the life of a creature is in the blood, and I have given it to you to make atonement for yourselves on the altar; it is the blood that makes atonement for one's life.

In the Old Testament, atonement was achieved by sacrificing animals of various types and values, according to the requirements of the ritual. This was normally done by appointed high priests and the priest's family. The reason for the atonement and the sacrifices of the animals in the Old Testament according to Leviticus 17:11 was that the blood, symbolizing life, represented the person's death as payment for his sin resulting in harmony and restoration between God and people or between individuals. Many theologians suggest that the sacrifices themselves did not possess any magical quality for removing sin, nor did they represent a payment to appease God. To the scholars, the objective of the atonement was based more on repentance, forgiveness, cleansing, and restoration. Ultimately, the entire process was a foreshadowing of what would take place thousands of years after the symbolism was initiated. Jesus was the one lamb who was slain to take away the sins of the entire world.

The Day of Atonement in the Old Testament was an important event in the lives of the Israelite people. God provided a way for his people to be worthy and exalted in his sight. On this day the high priest went into the Most Holy Place and sprinkled the blood of a bull and a goat on the atonement cover as a substitute for all people. The most dramatic event of the day followed the choosing of the scapegoat. Here, the priest would lay his hands on the head of the goat and confess the known and unknown sin habits, infractions, moral mistakes, and poor judgments of all the people. With this act he transferred the guilt onto the goat. A designated man would then lead the goat out into the wilderness never to return again...hopefully. If the goat ever returned to the camp, it would represent all the sins confessed and absolved returning to the people. That is why the Hebrew writing calls the sacrificial system imperfect but Jesus' sacrifice perfect. We never have to worry about our sins returning to us once we have been forgiven because Jesus was the perfect sacrifice. Our sins are totally removed as far as the east is from the west. We are separated from our sins by eternity (Psalm 103:12).

### Hebrews 9:6-15

[6] When everything had been arranged like this, the priests entered regularly into the outer room to carry on their ministry. [7] But only the high priest entered the inner room, and that only once a year, and never without blood, which he offered for himself and for the sins the people had committed in ignorance. [8] The Holy Spirit was showing by this that the way into the Most Holy Place had not yet been disclosed as long as the first tabernacle was still functioning. [9] This is an illustration for the present time, indicating that the gifts and sacrifices being offered were not able to clear the conscience of the worshiper. [10] They are only a matter of food and drink and various ceremonial washings—external regulations applying until the time of the new order.

## Atonement in the New Testament

The New Testament presents the person and sacrifice of Jesus of Nazareth as God's ultimate provision for atonement. In the New Testament Jesus Christ is the mediator between mankind and God the Father. "All this is from God, who reconciled us to himself through Christ and gave us the ministry of reconciliation" (2 Corinthians 5:18). In other words, the death of Christ was the total compensation for us as "sinners." Synonyms for "atonement" are amends, compensation, expiation, payment, redemption, and restitution. Combined, these words bring out nuances that one word alone misses. Jesus' blood redeemed our lives and made us useful. His blood paid a debt we couldn't pay. It made up for all the sins we committed because there was a righteous requirement that had to be met which was the loving act of the death of Jesus on the cross for mankind's sins. Jesus exchanged for us His righteousness for our sins. We received His holiness, and He received our sins in His body. He was punished or judged in our place. He died so we could live. He was given the death penalty for our crimes. Jesus was the atonement for our sins.

### 1 John 4:10

[10] This is love: not that we loved God, but that he loved us and sent his Son as an atoning sacrifice for our sins.

Matthew 20:28 reminds us that Jesus gave his life as "a ransom for many" and poured out his blood "for the forgiveness of sins" (Matt.26:28). The author of Hebrews emphasizes this point to make clear the doctrine of the purity of Christ as both the true and perfect sacrifice and the true and perfect priest who performs the ritual of atonement.

## Hebrews 8:3-6

[3] Every high priest is appointed to offer both gifts and sacrifices, and so it was necessary for this one also to have something to offer. [4] If he were on earth, he would not be a priest, for there are already priests who offer the gifts prescribed by the law. [5] They serve at a sanctuary that is a copy and shadow of what is in heaven. This is why Moses was warned when he was about to build the tabernacle: "See to it that you make everything according to the pattern shown you on the mountain." [6] But in fact the ministry Jesus has received is as superior to theirs as the covenant of which he is mediator is superior to the old one, since the new covenant is established on better promises.

The blood in the animal sacrifices of the Old Testament was a clear reminder that God required death as a punishment for every wrongdoing. Moreover, there was something further concerning the Old Testament atonement of animal sacrifices. The Day of Atonement pointed to a future event that had yet to occur. That future event happened on Good Friday with the death of Jesus Christ. Good Friday was *The* Day of Atonement. Jesus Christ was the atonement for the sins of all people for all time. It was this one-time event that did not need to be repeated every year. It was a one-time perfect sacrifice.

## Hebrews 10:10-12

[10] And by that will, we have been made holy through the sacrifice of the body of Jesus Christ once for all.
[11] Day after day every priest stands and performs his religious duties; again and again he offers the same sacrifices, which can never take away sins. [12] But when this priest had offered for all time one sacrifice for sins, he sat down at the right hand of God.

Did you read that? He *sat* down. His work was completed. We are redeemed. Our sins have been removed.

## Romans 8:1-4

[1] Therefore, there is now no condemnation for those who are in Christ Jesus, [2] because through Christ Jesus the law of the Spirit who gives life has set you free from the law of sin and death. [3] For what the law was powerless to do because it was weakened by the flesh, God did by sending his own Son in the likeness of sinful flesh to be a sin offering. And so he condemned sin in the flesh, [4] in order that the righteous requirement of the law might be fully met in us, who do not live according to the flesh but according to the Spirit.

# -Chapter 5-

# Doctrine of the Resurrection

Jesus' incarnation is also clearly designated as a fundamental doctrine: "Every spirit that confesses that Jesus Christ has come in the flesh is from God; and every spirit that does not confess Jesus is not from God; and this is the spirit of the antichrist" (1 John 4:2-3). "For many deceivers have gone out into the world, those who do not acknowledge Jesus Christ as coming in the flesh. This is the deceiver and the antichrist" (2 John 7). Those verses by implication also condemn those who deny the Virgin Birth of our Lord, for if He was not virgin-born, He would be merely human, not eternal God come in the flesh.

Jesus not only came into the word in human form, but He also suffered and died only to rise again. This key event of "rising from the dead" is what we mean when we refer to the resurrection. Understandably, the resurrection has been the subject of much debate. Of course, the bodily resurrection of Christ is a fundamental doctrine because 1 Corinthians 15:14 tells us, "If Christ has not been raised, our preaching is useless and so is your faith." Romans 10:9 confirms that the resurrection is a fundamental doctrine and adds another, the

Deity of Christ: "If you declare with your mouth, 'Jesus is Lord,' and believe in your heart that God raised him from the dead, you will be saved."

The two realities that Romans 10:9 declares is that Jesus is Lord or God and that God the Father raised Him from the dead. We will reverse the order and talk about the resurrection before we deal extensively with His deity. Was Jesus truly raised from the dead? Was there any evidence that He was just sedated and woke up later? Did the apostles make up the notion and did his followers naively believed it? Among other passages to cull to verify that Jesus was raised is 1 Corinthians 15: 1-56. Paul deals extensively on the topic for the skeptics of his day so that they may be assured of this truth. In other words the resurrection was not a small topic in Paul's time nor ours. It is a subject that must be totally understood and embraced. No Christian will have any security in his soul without a total affirmation of the authenticity of the resurrection.

## 1Corithians 15:1-8

[1] Now, brothers and sisters, I want to remind you of the gospel I preached to you, which you received and on which you have taken your stand. [2] By this gospel you are saved, if you hold firmly to the word I preached to you. Otherwise, you have believed in vain. [3] For what I received I passed on to you as of first importance: that Christ died for our sins according to the Scriptures, [4] that he was buried, that he was raised on the

third day according to the Scriptures, [5] and that he appeared to Cephas, and then to the Twelve. [6] After that, he appeared to more than five hundred of the brothers and sisters at the same time, most of whom are still living, though some have fallen asleep. [7] Then he appeared to James, then to all the apostles, [8] and last of all he appeared to me also, as to one abnormally born.

Not only is the resurrection an essential part of the gospel, but it has been confirmed by so many witnesses that any skeptic could have spoken to those who saw Jesus in order to verify it for themselves. Paul says that more than 500 people saw the resurrected Jesus and could attest to the truthfulness of the event. Even if someone could pay off several people to lie, none of the apostles were rich enough to pay that many people to lie. It was a verifiable fact that a very large group of people, Christians and non-Christians alike, saw the resurrected Jesus.

Paul was also a personal witness of the raised Jesus when Paul was on the road to Damascus on his way to persecute believers. This account recorded in Acts 9 describes the encounter that Paul had with Jesus who rebuked him for his misguided zeal. Jesus confronted Paul for persecuting Christians and told him that He took it personally. Repentant and bewildered, Paul had to come to grips with this challenge and came to embrace Jesus as Lord. Paul's life was turned upside down as believers reported: "The man who formerly persecuted us is now preaching the faith he once tried to destroy" (Galatians 1:23).

But was Jesus really dead or did He just faint and wake up 3 days later? For the answer to that question we have to go to a non-believer who witnessed the event.

### John 19:31-37

[31] Now it was the day of Preparation, and the next day was to be a special Sabbath. Because the Jewish leaders did not want the bodies left on the crosses during the Sabbath, they asked Pilate to have the legs broken and the bodies taken down. [32] The soldiers therefore came and broke the legs of the first man who had been crucified with Jesus, and then those of the other. [33] *But when they came to Jesus and found that he was already dead, they did not break his legs.* [34] *Instead, one of the soldiers pierced Jesus' side with a spear, bringing a sudden flow of blood and water.* [35] *The man who saw it has given testimony, and his testimony is true. He knows that he tells the truth, and he testifies so that you also may believe.* [36] These things happened so that the scripture would be fulfilled: "Not one of his bones will be broken," [37] and, as another scripture says, "They will look on the one they have pierced."

One of the soldiers who pierced Him shares that when Jesus was struck with a lance, blood and water flowed. Water and blood do not separate until a person is dead and for some time at that. So Jesus was not a few minutes dead when the soldier got to Him; He was dead for several hours. Did they make a mistake when they examined Him? If this were the case, they would have broken His legs like they did with the other two who were crucified along with Jesus. But that didn't happen because He was already found dead. The notion that Jesus passed out and awoke 3 days later was invented to try to dismiss the reality of the resurrection by those who didn't want to believe. What a ridiculous diversion to completely dismiss professionals who pretty much made their living crucifying people! They knew who was dead and who was not.

There was also a circulated story of the apostles stealing the body of Jesus in order to claim that He was raised from the dead. This is recorded in Matthew 28:11-15 right after the resurrection:

...some of the guards went into the city and reported to the chief priests everything that had happened. 12 When the chief priests had met with the elders and devised a plan, they gave the soldiers a large sum of money, 13 telling them, "You are to say, 'His disciples came during the night and stole him away while we were asleep.' 14 If this report gets to the governor, we will satisfy him and keep you out of trouble." 15 So the soldiers took the money and did as they were instructed. And this story has been widely circulated among the Jews to this very day.

The penalty for sleeping during a soldier's watch was death. The chief priests had to pay off two groups. They paid off the soldiers to keep the secret, and they had to pay off the governor so he wouldn't execute the soldiers who supposedly fell asleep. No such execution took place. The entire story was a fabrication to falsify the resurrection. It didn't work, however, because the eye-witnesses all paid with their lives (except John) for telling the truth. All the other apostles were executed according to church history. Peter was even crucified upside down. They couldn't kill John though, and it wasn't for the lack of trying. Extra biblical sources have it that they tried to boil him in oil but still couldn't kill him. So they banished him to the island of Patmos where he received the revelation we find at the end of the Bible that bears that name.

If the resurrection were a hoax, nobody in his right mind would die for it. If the disciples stole the body of Jesus or thought that Jesus fainted and came back to consciousness days later, they would not have given up their lives to sustain it. The only reasonable explanation for this total commitment to the resurrection story is that it really did happen. They knew it to be true, and they were willing to die for it. We can be sure of the resurrection because those who were the closest to Jesus knew it and affirmed it with their lives.

Even unbelievers knew the truth. The soldiers knew it because they were the first eye-witnesses of the event. The chief priests believed the story when the soldiers reported the events to them. I wonder if they would have paid with their lives to keep the truth from leaking out and if they would have denied the resurrection if a gun were pointed at their heads? Speculation aside, the resurrection was a true event in history. No doubt about it.

Since Jesus did truly rise from the dead, anyone who has placed his trust in Him can expect the same thing some day. The reason why we have hope is because of the certainty of Jesus' bodily resurrection. Without the resurrection of Jesus our faith falls apart. As Paul states, "If the dead are not raised, 'Let us eat and drink, for tomorrow we die" (1 Corinthians 15:32).

Mindless partying is justified if there is no resurrection. Eat, get drunk, and pursue bliss if there is no life after death and therefore no accountability to God. On the contrary because there is complete confidence in the resurrection of our bodies, we exercise self-control and live the life the Lord wants us to live. We want to live a life that is righteous and holy because we will see Him face to face. The resurrection of Jesus not only gives us hope but motivates us to holy living.

# -Chapter 6-

## Doctrine of the Deity of Jesus

### Romans 10:9

[9] If you declare with your mouth, "Jesus is Lord," and believe in your heart that God raised him from the dead, you will be saved.

Who is this Lord? Later in Romans 10:13 "for, 'Everyone who calls on the name of the LORD will be saved,'" is a quote from Joel 2:32. The reason why this quote is significant is because the Joel passage is actually referring to Yahweh God. Jesus is not just a supernatural being designated by God to redeem the world. He is God. If this one truth is not understood or completely embraced, everything else about the Christian faith will, in one way or another, fall apart.

To build on this reality we begin with the conversation that Moses had with Yahweh (refer to the glossary in Appendix A) in the book of Exodus: Moses said to God, "Suppose I go to the Israelites and say to them, 'The God of your fathers has sent me to you,' and they ask me, 'What is his name?' Then what shall I tell them?" God said to Moses, "I AM WHO I AM. This is what you are to say to the Israelites: '**I AM** has sent me to you.'" God also said to Moses, "Say to the

Israelites, 'The LORD, the God of your fathers—the God of Abraham, the God of Isaac, and the God of Jacob—has sent me to you.' This is my name forever, the name you shall call me from generation to generation"(Exodus 3:13-15).

God said His name is "I am" which in Hebrew is Yahweh. That means Jesus is the one who was talking with Moses in front of the burning bush. To confirm this with another passage so that we don't base our conclusion on only one text, we hear it from Christ's own words. When Jesus was having an argument about who belongs to whom, He rightly designates the unbelieving Jews as children of the devil and Himself as the Son of God, recorded in John 8: 42-44:

Jesus said to them, "If God were your Father, you would love me, for I have come here from God. I have not come on my own; God sent me. 43 Why is my language not clear to you? Because you are unable to hear what I say, 44 *you belong to your father, the devil*, and you want to carry out your father's desires. He was a murderer from the beginning, not holding to the truth, for there is no truth in him. When he lies, he speaks his native language, for he is a liar and the father of lies.

When Jesus claimed that He saw Abraham, their response was unbelief. At this point Jesus gave up His true identity by revealing who He was:

[57] "You are not yet fifty years old," they said to him, "and you have seen Abraham!"

[58] "Very truly I tell you," Jesus answered, "before Abraham was born, I am!" [59] At this, they picked up stones to stone him, but Jesus hid himself, slipping away from the temple grounds.

Jesus emphatically states that He is God. And if there was any misunderstanding about what Jesus was claiming, the response of the Jews confirmed it when they picked up stones to kill Him for blasphemy. He uttered those words. Nobody designated deity to Jesus before He said it. The angels who announced His coming to Mary said that He was Immanuel-God with us. This was a pun and did not fully reveal that Jesus was God. It only hinted to it. John the Baptist designated Jesus as the Lamb of God who takes away the sin of the world, and not as God Himself.

Jesus' true identity was veiled until He came to proclaim it Himself. Only then did His followers shout it from the rooftops. Just in case the Jews didn't get it the first time, He said it again in another way:

"I and the Father are one."

[31] Again his Jewish opponents picked up stones to stone him, [32] but Jesus said to them, "I have shown you many good works from the Father. For which of these do you stone me?"

<sup>33</sup> "We are not stoning you for any good work," they replied, "but for blasphemy, because you, a mere man, claim to be God." – John 10:30-33

This is the second time Jesus directly announced that He was God. It doesn't get any clearer than that. Even John in the opening summary of his gospel declares Jesus to be God.

<sup>1</sup> In the beginning was the Word, and the Word was with God, and the Word was God. <sup>2</sup> He was with God in the beginning. <sup>3</sup> Through him all things were made; without him nothing was made that has been made. <sup>4</sup> In him was life, and that life was the light of all mankind. <sup>5</sup> The light shines in the darkness, and the darkness has not overcome it (John1:1-5).

There is no question or vagueness in the Lord's own claim that He is truly deity.

Here is the big picture of salvation, and it is so well or-chestrated that we stand in awe of the plan of God. In order to have man created in His image, He had to have an image to model after. Jesus was that model. In order to redeem man, a perfect substitute had to be found. There was no one on earth found worthy to be that atoning sacrifice because "all have sinned and fall short of the glory of God" (Romans 3:23). There was only one in heaven who could do it. God Himself came to die on the cross to show the richest and the deepest love He has had since the beginning of creation. He could have used an angel or some other designated sacrifice and considered it good enough, but the supremacy of getting involved personally cannot be matched. Jesus being God is not only a proclamation from His own mouth, but also makes total sense in light of His redemptive plan for humanity. Therefore, worship Jesus with all your heart, soul, mind, and strength (Luke 10:27).

# -Chapter 7-

## Doctrine of the Trinity

Trinity is the central tenet of Christian theology in which the Father, the Son, and the Holy Spirit constitute one, personal, and triune God. The three persons in the Trinity are accepted as coequal, eternally self-existent, and mutually indwelling. The New Testament authors assumed the reality of the Trinity by describing all three persons as God.

When reading the Bible, you become aware that although God is "one" He is also "more than one" – God, Jesus, and the Holy Spirit. Together, they are referred to as the "Trinity" or the "Godhead." The "Godhead" are the distinct and co-equal persons of the Father, the Son, and the Holy Spirit. The Trinity share a fully divine essence of eternality, indivisibility, immutability (unchangeableness), omniscience (all knowing), omnipotence (all powerful), goodness, mercy, holiness, will and so forth. This makes each person fully God, yet with distinct roles.

In the work of the creation, the three persons of the Father, the Son, and the Holy Spirit had different functions. God the Father spoke the world into existence (Genesis 1-3), but God the son carried out the divine announcement. In the book of

John, the Bible tells us that all things were made through Jesus.

## John 1:3

[3] Through him all things were made; without him nothing was
made that has been made.

God the Holy Spirit was active in creation, "Now the earth
was formless and empty, darkness was over the surface of the
deep, and the Spirit of God was hovering over the waters"
(Genesis 1:2).

## Psalm 33:6

[6] By the word of the LORD the heavens were made,
their starry host by the breath of his mouth.

## Psalm 139:7

[7] Where can I go from your Spirit?
Where can I flee from your presence?

In the work of redemption, the Godhead had different roles
also. God the Father planned the redemption and sent God the
Son into the world to carry it out. Jesus obeyed the Father and
died on the cross. In John 14:26, we understand that the Holy
Spirit was sent by the Father and the Son to indwell every believer who receives the gift of salvation. God the Holy Spirit

then purifies and sanctifies each believer from the inside. Therefore, while the three persons of the Trinity share the same attributes, they have distinct functions as they relate to each other, creation, and the plan of salvation.

Remember, God is not so complex that He cannot be understood, but He cannot be understood totally either. The fact that He has no beginning is incomprehensible to created beings, but we accept it to be true because of the overwhelming evidence of the creation. The concept of Trinity is partly understandable and yet fully acceptable.

God is described as "one" in Deuteronomy 6:4, 1 Kings 8:60, Isaiah 44:8 and numerous other passages.

## Deuteronomy 6:4

[4] Hear, O Israel: The LORD our God, the LORD is one.

The Old Testament word "one" in Deuteronomy 6:4 is written in Hebrew as *'echad* (sound: ekh·äd'). This is the same Hebrew word that is used for "one" in Genesis 2:24: "That is why a man leaves his father and mother and is united to his wife, and they become **one** flesh." This does not indicate that when a man and woman marry, they become some sort of a mutant "one" flesh. They become "one" in essence but separate in their roles.

## Matthew 28:16-20

[16] Then the eleven disciples went to Galilee, to the mountain where Jesus had told them to go. [17] When they saw him, they worshiped him; but some doubted. [18] Then Jesus came to them and said, "All authority in heaven and on earth has been given to me. [19] Therefore go and make disciples of all nations, baptizing them in the name of the Father and of the Son and of the Holy Spirit, [20] and teaching them to obey everything I have commanded you. And surely I am with you always, to the very end of the age."

Matthew 28:16-20 is a passage referred to as "The Great Commission." In verse 19, Jesus states, "Therefore go and make disciples of all nations, baptizing them in the name of the Father and of the Son and of the Holy Spirit." Why would Jesus tell his eleven disciples to baptize people in the names of all three members of the Trinity? Why not just one or two? The Scriptures are clear from this passage that all the members of the Trinity are God, and the centrality of the doctrine of the Trinity is reinforced when from the outset new believers are baptized in the name of the three members.

# -Chapter 8-

## Doctrine of Salvation by Grace

Most world religions require the participant to work toward their salvation, nirvana, or paradise. In their eyes god or whatever represents their deity judges the progress of the worker and rewards him accordingly. The attainment of godhood, salvation, paradise, or nirvana depends upon what was done. All involve human beings accomplishing a task or set of tasks to achieve a rewardable goal. The tasks, goals, and rewards may vary, but the concept underlying all of them is the same – they are earned. However, in Christianity salvation is 100 percent the work of God. The thing that makes Christianity stand out from other religions is the concept of **grace**. As humans and because of our bondage to sin and rebellion, we do not have anything that will merit God's grace. God reached down to save mankind from sin and rebellion. His plan was simple – He sent His only Son to accomplish the greatest work for all mankind by crucifying Him on the cross. In John 19:30, Jesus said, "It is finished." The announcement is clear that all our sins are taken away. The wrath that we rightfully deserved has been placed upon Jesus.

Mankind deserves to be in prison being tortured for eternity, but Jesus came and paid our debts to set us free to worship God. As a part of the gift of salvation, believers become adopted as children of God. "So in Christ Jesus you are all children of God through faith" (Galatians 3:26). Now when we sin, God deals with us as a Father to a child (Hebrews 12:4-8). God's "grace" and actions are the determining factors in our salvation, including His work in our lives to develop a lifestyle consistent with salvation. As the creator God could have sent the entire human race to hell because they are "by nature deserving of wrath" (Ephesians 2:3), but God desired all to be saved: "This is good, and pleases God our Savior, [4] who wants all people to be saved and to come to a knowledge of the truth. [5] For there is one God and one mediator between God and mankind, the man Christ Jesus, [6] who gave himself as a ransom for all people" (1 Timothy 2:3-6). Although we deserved God's wrath, He exercised His "grace" toward us through Jesus Christ.

### Ephesians 2:4-10

[4] But because of his great love for us, God, who is rich in mercy, [5] made us alive with Christ even when we were dead in transgressions—it is by grace you have been saved. [6] And God raised us up with Christ and seated us with him in the heavenly realms in Christ Jesus, [7] in order that in the coming ages he might show the incomparable riches of his grace, expressed

in his kindness to us in Christ Jesus. [8] For it is by grace you have been saved, through faith—and this is not from yourselves, it is the gift of God— [9] not by works, so that no one can boast. [10] For we are God's handiwork, created in Christ Jesus to do good works, which God prepared in advance for us to do.

The apostle Paul helps us understand the importance of "no works" for salvation–"And if by grace, then it cannot be based on works; if it were, grace would no longer be grace" (Romans 11:6). Note, Paul is clearly separating "works" from "grace" and if anyone puts the slightest amount of "works" into the subject of salvation, then he has invalidated the meaning of grace because grace is unmerited favor. For grace to be grace we can't deserve it, and we don't deserve it. So then, how is a Christian a product of salvation by grace? The non-believer must first come to the realization that he needs a savior because of his sins. He then has to exercise faith that in Christ his sins will be removed (Romans 10:9-13), so he asks God to save him, and God saves him. Where is the work in that? Let us illustrate this in two ways:

You just got hired by a company to do work for them for an annual salary of $60,000. On your first day you get to work and go straight to your boss's office. You ask, "Please give me $60,000 because I need it!" Nobody in his right mind is going to give you a salary for asking. Asking is not the work. You have to produce. There must be labor.

On the other hand let's say you became a homeless person and were seriously ill. You go to the emergency room and tell the doctor, "I'm going to die if you don't do something. Please save me. But I don't have money to give you. I don't have any collateral because I don't own anything. I have nothing to offer you in exchange for the treatment." The doctor sees your condition and takes you in for emergency surgery and saves your life. Afterward, you thank him for being so kind and giving. Casually, he reports, "Oh no. It's not my kindness. It has nothing to do with me. Someone has donated money for this kind of situation. The reason why I operated on you is because someone else paid for your surgery by putting money into our emergency, non-paying-patients account. You had credit in your account because someone else put it there. God the Father saves us because Jesus put credit into our account. And asking is not considered work no more than asking for a salary before work began.

### Acts 16:30-31

[30] He then brought them out and asked, "Sirs, what must I do to be saved?" [31] They replied, "Believe in the Lord Jesus, and you will be saved-you and your household."

The Scriptures are clear that God requires no effort on our part to obtain salvation except to "believe in the Lord Jesus." This is a difficult principle to understand because all of us experientially expect "rewards" for good works, and know we don't deserve rewards without them. But what a blessing it is to know that we don't have to become perfect to be accepted by God because if perfection was the requirement, nobody would be qualified to go to heaven. This is why salvation only produces gratitude, praise, and obedience. When someone gives you a gift you can't purchase at a cost that would be impossible to pay, all you can do is say, "Thank you," for the rest of eternity. You can't pay God back for your salvation so thank Him all the time. What a marvelous gift! Be devoted to Him for the rest of your life, praise and thank Him continually, and respond to Him in obedience.

### Romans 1:5
5 Through him we received grace and apostleship to call all the Gentiles to the obedience that comes from faith for his name's sake.

### 2 Corinthians 6:1
1 As God's co-workers we urge you not to receive God's grace in vain.

## 1 Corinthians 15:10

[10] But by the grace of God I am what I am, and his grace to me was not without effect. No, I worked harder than all of them — yet not I, but the grace of God that was with me.

Obedience is a natural product of God's grace. Why would we not want to follow the one who saved our lives? The doctor who saved the homeless man's life should be getting birthday cards and Christmas presents every year at the least. And if you were the homeless man and the doctor ever asked you for anything, you would make every effort to meet his request. Give God your complete loyalty and obedience.

## Romans 3:21-24

[21] But now apart from the law the righteousness of God has been made known, to which the Law and the Prophets testify. [22] This righteousness is given through faith in Jesus Christ to all who believe. There is no difference between Jew and Gentile, [23] for all have sinned and fall short of the glory of God, [24] and all are justified freely by his grace through the redemption that came by Christ Jesus.

Our Father in heaven has devised a great plan for all mankind to stand righteous before Him. God has sent His own Son as a sacrifice on our behalf, and those who believe in Him shall have everlasting life, and shall be seen as righteous in God's sight. This is all by grace. We didn't do a single thing to deserve it. On the contrary we did everything to deserve eternal punishment. But God's grace is so much greater that it superseded all our sins. That's how salvation came to us-by grace.

# -Chapter 9-

# Confirm the Faith

Before continuing we would like to rejoice with you in becoming a follower of Jesus Christ. Your decision to accept Him as your Lord and Savior is the most important decision you could ever make a decision that has eternal consequences. You have been relocated from the dominion of darkness into His marvelous light. Your citizenship is now in heaven. Welcome to the body of believers! You are now our sibling. Whatever your past may have been and no matter how many sins you have committed, God has wiped your slate clean because you have turned from your sins and embraced Jesus Christ as your redeemer.

In the past, when you did not know God, you were spiritually dead. Ephesians 2:1 says, "As for you, you were dead in your transgressions and sins." All of us were born with a physical body, but spiritually we were dead. Death does not mean what we normally think of when we think of death. A better word for death is separation. Being dead in our transgressions and sins means we have been separated from our relationship with God because of our sinful nature. When we say that a marriage is dead, we don't mean that the couple died. We are saying that the relationship is irreparable.

The couple is living 2 separate lives. It is a complete separation of the relationship. Spiritual death is our separation from God. We don't have a relationship with God when we are dead in sin (Sin in the singular can mean two things: one sin we commit or sin as a principle. We mean the latter here). We don't have a desire for Him, and He can't relate with us because our sins are getting in the way of His holiness. However, by repenting and placing your faith in Christ, you went from death to life, from no relationship to an eternal standing with God as His child. The apostle Paul said if you are "in Christ," you are a brand new creature (2 Corinthians 5:17) and you have been born into God's family.

God has been watching over you before you were even born. Jeremiah 1:5 says, "Before I formed you in the womb I knew you, before you were born I set you apart; I appointed you as a prophet to the nations." God knew you, as He knew Jeremiah, long before you were born or even conceived. He thought about you and planned a destiny for you. When you feel discouraged or inadequate, remember that God has always loved you and valued you. The God who made the universe prepared it with you in mind. The universe was made for us. How amazing is that? The longing in his heart was to have a relationship with those He created.

### Matthew 23:37

"Jerusalem, Jerusalem, you who kill the prophets and stone

those sent to you, *how often I have longed to gather your children together, as a hen gathers her chicks under her wings,* and you were not willing.

Have you ever pondered these questions?

- *Why would an "Almighty God" care about me?*
- *Why would God want a relationship with me?*
- *Does God really have a purpose and plan for my life?*

Once you know the answers to these questions, you will experience a radical change in your life because "The truth will set you free" (John 8:32). Your personal decision to surrender your life to God started a journey toward being a fully devoted follower of Jesus Christ. You will experience new levels of freedom and a transformation only God can bring. God will change your life. And you will be changed because God is going to work in you. He is not an absentee father who doesn't interact with His children. He will conform you into the image of His Son. Furthermore, Jesus is going to live His life in you through the Holy Spirit. We call Jesus our Lord because we have surrendered our control over to Him. When we submit to Him in this way, we become a member of His family. John expressed this in his gospel, "But to all who did receive him, who believed in his name, he gave the right to become children of God" (John 1:12). Because you received Jesus Christ as your Lord, you became God's child.

From this point on, you will have some exciting and challenging days ahead of you. As you communicate with your heavenly Father through prayer, He will answer and guide you in everything you do. He will transform you into the person He wants you to be. You will be amazed at the changes that will take place. At the same time as you endeavor to live for Him, Satan will make every attempt to distract you from getting closer to Him. Satan can't oppose God so he tries to come against the objects of His love. You are Satan's target. He's been targeting God's people from the beginning. In the book of Genesis we read that Satan persuaded the first man Adam to disobey God. Satan accomplished this by deceiving Adam's wife Eve. This deception paved the way for the devil to control the whole human race.

## Ephesians 2:1-2

[1] As for you, you were dead in your transgressions and sins, [2] in which you used to live when you followed the ways of this world and of the ruler of the kingdom of the air, the spirit who is now at work in those who are disobedient.

The world as a system is ruled by Satan. You were once a pawn on his board. However, your acceptance of Jesus Christ as Lord delivered you from Satan's control. He no longer has authority over you because you belong to God's family now. Let's use adoption as an illustration:

Your natural spiritual father was Satan, and he mistreated you and used you as a tool for his evil schemes. Under his fatherhood you lied, stole, cheated, murdered, lusted, fornicated, coveted, and pursued selfish ambitions. You thought you had no choice because nothing else was offered to you. Along comes God the Father who says, "I will never mistreat you or compel you to do evil. Would you like to become my adopted child? All you have to do is say, 'Yes,' and you will forever be mine. You'll never have to worry about Satan hurting you again."

"What about the cost of adoption?" you ask, "and what about all the crimes I've committed?"

God the Father understandingly replies, "I will pay the cost of the adoption, and since I have the executive prerogative to forgive, I will remove all records of all the crimes you have committed. You will truly be free."

"It sounds too good to be true. Who in his right mind would do such a thing for me? I don't deserve any of it. How can I know what you are saying to me is true?" you inquire in disbelief.

"Try it. Say, yes," He replies.

You take a while but you decide to take a chance since you don't have anything to lose. You're tired of the life you were living so you say, "Yes."

God comes over to your house and puts a ring on your finger indicating that you are His. As you're walking out the door Satan runs over and grabs your arm in fuming anger, demanding an explanation of why God is taking you with Him. God breaks his grip and tells him that you said, "Yes," to His offer. And as you two walk away from your house, Satan shouts in defiance, "I'll get you back if it's the last thing I do." But God confidently comforts you with, "He'll never get you back. This transaction is permanent, and you belong to me now, and I'll never let you go."

Thereafter, your new Father wipes your slate clean and places you in His home. But frequently Satan comes to your fence in your new home and calls out, "You're mine. You will always be mine. You have to listen to me. You must go home with me." And others come demanding that you must go to jail for committing all kinds of crimes. You feel guilty about everything, but your heavenly Father reminds you He paid it all. You are safe with Him and you don't have to listen to your old spiritual father anymore. You can begin to build a relationship with your new Father who adopted you permanently.

From the illustration you can see how just by knowing you belong to another breaks the old relational habits. When sin or Satan says you must do something, you don't have to obey. God expressed his remedy for sin in 1 John 3:8, "Whoever makes a practice of sinning is of the devil, for the devil has been sinning from the beginning. The reason the Son of God appeared was to destroy the works of the devil." Remember that Satan will act like you are still his child. But he has no power over you. He has bark but no bite. Rest assured that you have been set free from evil and empowered to be righteous.

## Understanding and Confirming Your Salvation

Let us begin by first understanding the word "sinner." The Bible helps us understand that the sinner is not necessarily a horrible, hateful person but a person who has chosen NOT to journey through life trusting in God. The "sin" is normally an act or thought that deliberately violates divine law and opposes God's holiness. All of us were born as "sinners" and therefore fall short of the righteousness required by a holy God. This is the sole reason why Jesus died on the cross for us, so that He could bridge the gap between the "sinner" and the righteous God. The word "repent" simply means that you have decided to ask God to forgive your sins so that you can start to walk with God instead of against Him. The repentant person acknowledges his own sins and determines not to sin again.

# Confirming Your Salvation through Scripture

<u>You</u> agreed with God that you were a sinner and that your sin was separating you from Him.

### Romans 3:23

23 for all have sinned and fall short of the glory of God,

<u>God</u> brought you to the realization that there was nothing that you could do (good conduct, good works or religious acts) to save yourself from the penalty of sin. You transferred your trust from what you have been doing to what Jesus Christ has done for you on the cross to pay the penalty for your sins.

### Ephesians 2:8-9

8For by grace you have been saved through faith. And this is not your own doing; it is the gift of God, 9 not a result of works, so that no one may boast.

### Romans 6:23

23 For the wages of sin is death, but the gift of God is eternal life in Christ Jesus our Lord.

<u>You</u> accepted Jesus Christ as Lord and Savior and believed that God has raised him from the dead.

## Romans 10:9-10

[9]because, if you confess with your mouth that Jesus is Lord and believe in your heart that God raised him from the dead, you will be saved. [10]For with the heart one believes and is justified, and with the mouth one confesses and is saved.

## Romans 10:13

[13] for, "Everyone who calls on the name of the Lord will be saved."

**You** repented of your sins and accepted God's forgiveness.

## Acts 3:19

[19] Repent, then, and turn to God, so that your sins may be wiped out, that times of refreshing may come from the Lord,

## Psalm 103:12

[12] as far as the east is from the west,
so far has he removed our transgressions from us.

**God** promises you a personal relationship with Jesus Christ. Here's what the Bible says about your new life in Jesus Christ. The following are some of God's promises in the Bible:

## 2 Corinthians 5:17

[17]Therefore, if anyone is in Christ, he is a new creation. The old has passed away; behold, the new has come.

<u>You</u> cannot lose your personal relationship with Jesus Christ.

### John 10:27-30

[27]My sheep hear my voice, and I know them, and they follow me. [28]I give them eternal life, and they will never perish, and no one will snatch them out of my hand. [29]My Father, who has given them to me, is greater than all, and no one is able to snatch them out of the Father's hand. [30] I and the Father are one."

<u>You</u> can know beyond a shadow of doubt that you have a personal relationship with Jesus Christ.

### 1 John 5:10-12

[10]Whoever believes in the Son of God has the testimony in himself. Whoever does not believe God has made him a liar, because he has not believed in the testimony that God has borne concerning his Son. [11]And this is the testimony that God gave us eternal life, and this life is in his Son. [12] Whoever has the Son has life; whoever does not have the Son of God does not have life.

<u>God</u> lives inside of you in the person of the Holy Spirit. You have received the Holy Spirit and have been sealed by Him who will lead you into all truth.

### John 14:16-17

<sup>16</sup>And I will ask the Father, and he will give you another Hel per, to be with you forever, <sup>17</sup>even the Spirit of truth, whom the world cannot receive, because it neither sees him nor knows him. You know him, for he dwells with you and will be in you.

### Ephesians 1:13-14

<sup>13</sup>In him you also, when you heard the word of truth, the gospel of your salvation, and believed in him, were sealed with the promised Holy Spirit, <sup>14</sup>who is the guarantee of our inheritance until we acquire possession of it, to the praise of his glory.

## New Creation

When you accepted Jesus Christ into your heart, you became a new creation with the desire to live a new life. Now, you love God and want to obey Him. Your motives changed like Paul's:

### Galatians 2:20

<sup>20</sup> I have been crucified with Christ and I no longer live, but Christ lives in me. The life I now live in the body, I live by faith in the Son of God, who loved me and gave himself for me.

In becoming a Christian the Bible says your very nature, the essence of who you are, changed. 2 Corinthians 5:17 states,

"Therefore, if anyone is in Christ, the new creation has come: The old has gone, the new is here!" The "new creation" is the Spirit that lives inside of you as God promised He will "give you a new heart and put a new spirit in you" (Ezekiel 36:26). The transformation happened inside of you when you surrendered your "old you" and received a "new you." Now our new spirit endeavors to honor and worship the one who made us new.

The Bible tells us that man has three fundamental components of existence. Each of us is made up of the spirit, soul, and body. Our body is the temple that holds the Spirit given to us by God. "Do you not know that your bodies are temples of the Holy Spirit, who is in you, whom you have received from God? You are not your own" (1 Corinthians 6:19). The soul is the part of us that expresses emotions and reason, while the spirit is our moral conscience, distinguishing between right and wrong. As a believer in Christ, you are indwelt by the Holy Spirit so in addition to your own body, soul, and spirit, you now have God's Spirit living in you. When the Holy Spirit came to live in you, you were born again; you then become a child God's spiritual child. In John 3:3 Jesus replied, "Very truly I tell you, no one can see the kingdom of God unless he is born again."

You now recognize God's presence in your life, for you sense His displeasure whenever you fall back into sin. But rather than justifying or ignoring it which you used to do when you didn't know God, you will repent and turn away from it. Repentance is a sign that the Holy Spirit is working in you. Repentance is deep sorrow or regret for having sinned, then a change of heart toward righteousness. Sin is an offence to God, a violation of His holy law; therefore, repentance is a movement toward God which inevitably results in a changed life because God affects the change.

## Acts 11:18

18 When they heard this, they had no further objections and praised God, saying, "So then, even to Gentiles God has granted repentance that leads to life."

Our Father in heaven has accepted you and forgiven you of your sins on account of Christ's sacrifice on the cross which means the penalty of your sins is fully paid for. God accepted Jesus' sacrifice as payment for your sins and has settled your account with God. When you turned to Christ in genuine repentance and put your faith in Him, by grace and mercy God granted you an eternal relationship with Him. Praise the Lord for His abundant love, and welcome to the Family.

# Part 3

# Prayer

The very first thing people told me to do in prayer was "just talk to God." This principle of just talking to God did not help me in my prayer life, nor did it develop any personal relationship with Jesus because I (Joseph) just didn't know how to talk to Him. I couldn't develop any intimacy with God and felt frustrated because I didn't know what God wanted from me. In prayer we get to know God better, and He reveals Himself to us. It is a two-way communication medium that is more intimate than a physical relationship with the opposite gender. It doesn't happen very often but when two people are really communicating their heart, there is a bonding that takes place that is really difficult to break. The value of the communication is determined by the level of sharing that takes place. Sharing that we ate pancakes for breakfast is less intimate than sharing whom we like as a girlfriend, but even more intimate is admitting that we proposed to someone and got rejected. Sometimes the subject doesn't have to be considered consequential to be deep. I (Jae) had a childhood dream of building my own house. It was

3

Prayer

something that I only shared when I was young with my best friend. It may even seem trivial to the average person who had many such dreams, but for me it was very dear so to share it would mean that I was revealing myself, the greater the disclosure of self the greater the indication of trust and desire for a connection.

Intimacy is not defined by service or busyness in doing Christian activities. Bible study, worship attendance, fasting, evangelism, and so forth are all important Christian "activities," but they are never intended to be a substitute for a relationship with God but merely some of the means by which the relationship can be experienced. The ultimate purpose of prayer, however, is to cultivate that intimacy by getting to know Him better. God desires to communicate with us and disclose Himself so that we can know Him better.

### John 17:3

Now this is eternal life: that they know you, the only true God, and Jesus Christ, whom you have sent.

### John 14:21

The one who loves me will be loved by my Father, and I too will love them and show myself to them.

During the early years of my Christian life, I (Joseph) learned how to pray by listening to others. However, by that method I could only pray for about five minutes, max, unlike some amazing prayer warriors who could pray for two to three hours a day. My prayers seemed very robotic and emotionless. "What in the world could they be praying about?" I thought. It's no wonder why God did not answer all my half-hearted prayers, and when He did, it was only because of His grace knowing that I was a mere infant in Christ.

I am not a free spirited type that can just bring up a lot of subjects and make different types of petitions to God. My mind works in a very logical and practical way, where I literally need someone to say, "O.k. Mr. Choi! You need to take step number 1 and once you do this, then go to step number 2." That's how my mind is wired.

One time I had to go out to the grocery store and get some medication for my son who had a fever, but before I left my wife actually had to write the name of the medication with a drawing of the bottle so I wouldn't buy the wrong one. Would you believe even with that note I still had to call my wife and verify it once more? It truly helps when people are able to hold your hand and guide you through the practice of prayer.

Because praying was difficult, I actually asked God to teach me how to pray. That seemed like a no-brainer, but having asked how to pray, I had to search the Bible to help me understand the basic principles, concepts, and methods of prayer. Although by no means exhaustive, this is what I found.

**WHAT PRAYER IS NOT**: When you pray to a Holy God who created the universe, don't rush into His presence to demand something, or make a deal, or put conditions on Him for the answers. People will say, "Jesus, if you help me with this, then I will do this for you." Or they pray, "God, I will give my time and money, but You need to do such and such for me." And some people think God will do whatever they ask if they pray for a long time. Don't dishonor God by doing that. Did you need to ask your father for the car keys for 2 hours? If you were hungry, did you ask your mom for 15 minutes for something to eat? Did manipulation ever work on your parents? If your parents were discerning, you never got your way through cunning? How much smarter do you think God is? *Praying to Almighty God is an opportunity to magnify Him* so come into His presence recognizing who God is and what He can do for you.

The Almighty and Holy God is your Father so using the model of the Lord's Prayer can help you enter His family room to bring your concerns, hurts, and needs; however, you will need to enter with reverence and fear because He is also the King of kings and Lord of lords who demands obedience and loyalty.

**Short Answers**: How to Pray

**Step 1**: Read the Lord's Prayer in Matthew 6:9 - 13 or memorize the A.C.T.S. principle in chapter 12.

**Step 2**: Establish a Daily Prayer Time and stay consistent and persistent, except for Sundays.

**Step 3**: Determine an Amount of Time to Pray. Start small and build up. You will discover over time that you never have enough time.

**Step 4**: Find a Consistent Place to Pray

**Step 5**: Pray through Matthew 6:9–13

**Step 6**: Pray from your heart

**Step 7**: Listen while praying

**Step 8**: Journal your prayers for the first 30 days

**Key Note:** Remember if you do not know how to pray then ask the Holy Spirit to help you (Romans 8:26).

# -Chapter 10-

## Importance of Prayer

For close to a year, I prayed through Matthew 6:9-13 and learned amazing things which I used to take for granted. Eventually, learning the basics of prayer helped me through college; it helped me find a career and my wife; it helped me understand what it meant to be a husband, a father, a leader, and most importantly prayer helped strengthen me in times of trials and tribulations. Why would such a holy God answer your prayers? It is because you have a personal relationship with Him through Jesus Christ. You are a child of God, and He loves you.

**Romans 8:16**

[16] The Spirit himself testifies with our spirit that we are God's children.

How important is prayer? Prayer was so important that it was the last thing Jesus taught his disciples before he died. If you knew you were going to die the next day, what would you teach your disciples? Jesus chose prayer as His legacy, and it continues to this very day, even to you.

## Matthew 26:36

[36] Then Jesus went with his disciples to a place called Gethsemane, and he said to them, "Sit here while I go over there and pray."

Jesus knew that he would die the next day, so he took his disciples to a place called Gethsemane to pray (Matt. 26:36), but when he returned to his disciples, he found them sleeping "Couldn't you men keep watch with me for one hour?" he asked (Matt. 26:40). Jesus told the disciples to "watch and pray" and again in verse 41. Later, Jesus returned to find them sleeping again, "So he left them and went away once more and prayed the third time, saying the same thing" (Matt. 26:44).

If prayer was paramount to Jesus' life and ministry, then it must be a priority for us too. Prayers are recorded throughout the Old Testament, John the Baptist taught his disciples to pray, and the disciples of Jesus realized that they needed to be taught how to pray so they asked:

## Luke 11:1

[1] One day Jesus was praying in a certain place. When he finished, one of his disciples said to him, "Lord, teach us to pray, just as John taught his disciples."

What Jesus taught them was not a prayer to be memorized and recited as a ritual. It was a prayer guideline, format or structure for the disciples to build on. God wants meaningful dialogue with us and isn't interested in routine or vain repetition. In fact, God seeks those who worship Him in sincerity and truth. Our relationship with Him must be totally genuine and intimately personal. You don't want someone to talk to you like a robot. Neither does the Lord.

**Matthew 6:7**

[7] And when you pray, do not keep on babbling like pagans, for they think they will be heard because of their many words.

God wants a close, personal relationship with each of us. Knowing how to pray will not come naturally for most new believers; it will take time, consistency, and patience but most importantly a driving passion to seek God's face. The "Lord's Prayer" is a framework for every kind of praying. In the beginning of your prayer journey, it will be helpful to memorize key words until you feel comfortable enough to move to the next level. So rather than repeating the Lord's Prayer verbatim, you can address your concerns by topics. Remember, Jesus tells us not to ramble on during prayer. He knows what's on our hearts. Our words should be few. The effective prayer is not measured by how loud you pray, or how long you pray, but how submissive and sincere you are. Proverbs 16:2 tell us,

"All a person's ways seem pure to them, but motives are weighed by the LORD."

---

### *Matthew 6:9-13*

[9] "This, then, is how you should pray:

"'Our Father in heaven,
hallowed be your name,
[10] your kingdom come,
your will be done,
on earth as it is in heaven.
[11] Give us today our daily bread.
[12] And forgive us our debts,
as we also have forgiven our debtors.
[13] And lead us not into temptation,
but deliver us from the evil one.'

---

Is that it? It seems so short and simple. Don't be fooled. Jesus was introducing to his disciples the basics, but there's a lot of meat on those bones. As the disciples matured and grew to better understand these primary concepts, they learned to pray more effectively. But most importantly they learned how to relate with their heavenly Father in the most intimate and appropriate way. They saw the Lord move in ways that even went beyond some of the things the Lord did on earth (John 14:12, Acts 2:41).

**Short Answers**: Relationships in
The Lord's Prayer (Matthew 6:9–13)

**"Our Father"**: Father and Child

**"Hallowed be your name"**: God and Worshiper

**"Your Kingdom come"**: King and Subject

**"Your will be done"**: Master and Servant

**"Give us ... bread"**: Provider and Recipient

**"Forgive us our debts (sins)"**: Savior and Sinner

**"Lead us not into temptation"**: Leader and
Follower

**"Deliver us from evil"**: Protector and Deliverer

As you can see Christ was teaching the disciples the different aspects of our relationship with the Father. In every line of the prayer there is a relationship emphasized. It begins with a familial connection and ends with a deliverer tie. We relate to God in all these ways. We have a role in the dialogue. Through prayer there is an appropriate interaction taking place between God and us. You may not see it in the prayer, but God is responding back to the believer. You would be surprised how often He speaks to us when we pray. We'll see how that happens in the next chapter.

**Short Answers**: Primary Points in Prayer

**Point 1**: The supreme purpose of prayer is to honor and glorify God.

**Point 2**: Prayer is an opportunity for God to manifest His goodness and glory to the believers.

**Point 3**: If you do not know how to pray then ask the Holy Spirit to help you.

**Romans 8:26**
26 In the same way, the Spirit helps us in our weakness. We do not know what we ought to pray for, but the Spirit himself intercedes for us through wordless groans.

# Chapter 11

# Understanding the Lord's Prayer

Jesus said, "When you pray, say Our Father..." What an incredible privilege it is to dialogue with our Great God! King David, when still a shepherd boy looking up at the stars, thought it was remarkable that the Almighty Creator God would even take the time to think of man. He wrote in Psalms 8:3-4: "When I consider your heavens, the work of your fingers, the moon and the stars, which you have set in place, 4 what is mankind that you are mindful of them, human beings that you care for them?"

We state "Our Father" to affirm the relationship and our dependence upon Him. This is not an employer-employee relationship. We don't say, "Hey boss, what can I do for you today?" We are a family. We need Him, and He wants to build us up, lead us, and provide for us. When He answers our prayers, He is bringing glory to Himself.

**John 14:13**

13 And I will do whatever you ask in my name, so that the Father may be glorified in the Son.

Now, Jesus was inviting the disciples to have a father-son relationship with God instead of just a master-slave kind. This was more than they could comprehend. Because the Old Testament rarely referred to God as Father, the disciples found it difficult to address God in this way. But Jesus insisted that the disciples connect with God as a loving Father. He gave the disciples the relationship He had with the Father. For over three years, Jesus modeled for them the kind of personal relationship they should pursue with the Father.

## The Lord's Prayer:

### Matthew 6:9-13

[9] "This, then, is how you should pray:

"'Our Father in heaven,
hallowed be your name,
[10] your kingdom come,
your will be done,
on earth as it is in heaven.
[11] Give us today our daily bread.
[12] And forgive us our debts,
as we also have forgiven our debtors.
[13] And lead us not into temptation,
but deliver us from the evil one.'

**Brief Summary:** The Lord's Prayer contains two sections. The first section deals with God's glory (vv. 9-10) and the second with man's need (vv. 11-13). Furthermore, each section is composed of three petitions (appeals or requests). The first three are petitions on behalf of God's name, His Kingdom, and His will. The second three are petitions for daily bread, forgiveness, and protection from temptation. Jesus didn't tell the disciples, "This is **what** you should pray." Instead He told them **"This, then, is *how* you should pray."** The disciples did not ask Jesus to teach them a prayer but to teach them "how" to pray. To paraphrase Jesus was saying, "Pray then, in this way," or "Pray along these lines."

**Our Father in heaven:** The Almighty God is "Our Father," who is worthy of our adoration, praise, and honor. There is no earthly father like He. Therefore, as believers, we are to pray to our Father with a childlike respect, love, and confidence. "In Heaven," are all the resources that are available to us when we trust God as our heavenly supplier, but we must seek the giver of gifts and not just the gifts. It would be inappropriate and dishonoring to approach our heavenly Father for all the things He could provide and not want to have anything to do with Him.

**Hallowed be your name:** Another word for "hallowed" is "holy." So, when saying, "hallowed be your name" in essence you are saying, "Let Your name be holy on earth as it is holy in heaven." Even the angel's cried out "Holy, holy, holy is the Lord Almighty; the whole earth is full of his glory" (Isaiah 6:3). Therefore, when you pray "Hallowed be your name," you are treating God with the adoration, respect, and honor that He deserves. We are saying to the Creator that He deserves the utmost worship, and we do this by honoring His name because His name is who He is.

**Your kingdom come:** God is the King over His dominion, and the King is inseparable from His kingdom. When we pray "Your kingdom come," we are recognizing that God is the ruler of our lives, and we want to see Him, ruling over the entire world. And if He is the King, we are His subjects, privileged to serve Him in any way He commands. We ought to be constantly concerned with applying His "kingdom" principles in our daily lives. All that is good and right about heaven is what we want on earth. His rule, His presence, His joy, and His fellowship are all included in the plea.

**Your will be done, on earth as it is in heaven:** This aspect of prayer is affirming your submission to God's plan for your life. When you say "Your will be done," you are praying first that God's will become your will and not only that but that His will be the only will on "earth as it is in heaven." What is the point of declaring supremacy of His will? Our will and His will are in conflict in an on-going battle. If we don't remind ourselves that we are serving Him instead of the other way around, we will live like He exists for us. We can never forget that we exist for Him. We have joined His cause so we follow His plan. We must have no will of our own. We must do everything that pleases Him (John 8:29).

[For further understanding of God's Will for your life, go to Part 5: "Knowing God's Will"]

**Give us today our daily bread:** The word "bread" is a symbol that stands for all our physical needs. It is breathtaking to understand that a Holy and Mighty God that created the universe and who is completely self-sufficient, would even consider caring and supplying our physical needs. How wonderful it is that we should know a God that truly provides. Just think how much you would care about your children's needs. Now multiply that by a million. That doesn't even come close to how much He cares about your needs. Do you think He will provide those needs?

### Matthew 6:32-33

[32] For the pagans run after all these things, and your heavenly Father knows that you need them. [33] But seek first his kingdom and his righteousness, and all these things will be given to you as well.

**And forgive us our debts, as we also have forgiven our debtors:** The principle behind this process is that as a child of God, you are simply saying "I am sorry Lord for the wrong (sin) I have done. Please forgive me." Repentance from the heart restores the fellowship we have with the Father. (A distinction needs to be made here between a relationship and fellowship. We make this distinction for this section only because sometimes the word relationship is used synonymously with the word fellowship, as in a good relationship or a bad relationship with another person.) Fellowship occurs in the context of a relationship. Once we become believers we have a relationship with God that never changes. We are His children forever. But our fellowship with our heavenly Father can have its ups and downs like our human relationships.

When I (Jae) offend my wife, I may end up on the couch because our fellowship is broken, but our relationship or marriage doesn't change unless we get a divorce. A more permanent illustration is with my son. If we have broken our fellowship in one way or another, we can restore that fellowship by apologizing and forgiving, but our relationship will never change in a zillion years. We will be father-son forever.

All of our sins have been wiped clean, past, present, and future, because of the cross. We suffer no eternal consequences because of our sins. We only suffer fellowship-wise if we don't repent. Therefore, we seek forgiveness in order to be renewed in our fellowship with the Father. Sin that is not confessed is not forgiven (1 John 1:9). We may get away with it when relating to people, but not with God. And, since sin separates us from God, forgiveness restores the fellowship in the case of the believer and in the case of the unbeliever forgiveness begins his relationship with the Father. Get used to repenting because you never want anything to hinder your fellowship with the Father.

The condition attached to asking for forgiveness attests to the seriousness of God's concern for our fellowship with other people. If we don't forgive others, God won't forgive us which means our unwillingness to forgive others keeps our fellowship with the Father from being restored. Then, we can never have fellowship with God without restoring our fellowship with others. It cannot get any clearer than that.

### Matthew 6:14-15

[14] For if you forgive other people when they sin against you, your heavenly Father will also forgive you. [15] But if you do not forgive others their sins, your Father will not forgive your sins.

This stands to reason. If Jesus came to earth for the purpose of providing forgiveness for mankind, then it is the most important agenda God has. What would it say about us if we say we want Your forgiveness God, but other people can't have ours? We're not saying "Your will be done." But that's what we consented to in the beginning of our prayer. When it comes to forgiveness, be as generous as your heavenly Father is, and He will bless you with sweet fellowship with Him.

**And lead us not into temptation:** First and foremost, we must understand that God does not lead anyone into a situation to be induced to commit sin, nor would a Holy God tempt anyone. "When tempted, no one should say, 'God is tempting me. 'For God cannot be tempted by evil, nor does he tempt anyone" (James 1:13). After rebirth the heart desire of the believer is to avoid sin and the consequences that follow. It happens naturally as the result of the Spirit's indwelling presence, which means that temptation is now greater and the fight more intense. We feel threatened by sin. Our awareness of what displeases God increases so we have to be more diligent about being pure. This is why we pray, "Steer us away from temptation." We don't want to be in its proximity. We don't even want a whiff. We never want to sin against God by falling into temptation. We only want to honor and glorify Him.

**But deliver us from the evil one:** When you accepted Jesus Christ as Lord over your life and you surrendered your heart to the Father, Satan lost another one. I don't know about you, but I hate losing. Imagine a greedy, selfish, egotistical, hedonist, of the worst kind losing a prized possession to somebody else. Do you think he's going to sit around and accept defeat maturely? Consequently, expect a tenacious fight to get you back or at least expect Satan to try to destroy the fellowship you have with the Father. Before you came under the headship of Christ, your conscience and heart had a shallow understanding of wrongdoing; however, after accepting Christ your mind and heart were touched by the Spirit of God's holiness. Satan is going to fight against that desire for holiness tooth and nail so you're going to need God's help to withstand him. Nobody on earth and in heaven has the capacity to defeat Satan except the Lord. Only He can deliver us. But in order for God to "deliver us from the evil one," we must be under His protection and submit to His Word. "Submit yourselves, then, to God. Resist the devil, and he will flee from you" (James 4:7). We are confessing our need for protection and deliverance to our protective Father and we don't fear the evil one because we have one greater than He who holds us in His hand (Deut. 31:12, 1John 4:4). We are sober about Satan's power, but we don't fear him. God holds our destiny in His hands and not the evil one. He will subdue Satan and deliver us from him.

### 1 Peter 5:9

9 Resist him, standing firm in the faith, because you know that the family of believers throughout the world is undergoing the same kind of sufferings.

## Sample of How You Can Put the Lord's Prayer together:

**"Our Father in heaven"** you are the Almighty God, who deserves all honor, all praise, and all glory. You created heaven and earth and you created me because you loved me. So, **"Hallowed be your name"** by which I was saved from sin and came into your presence. May your name be lifted up by the way I conduct myself. Father may, **"Your kingdom come."** Rest in my heart and rule over it as your dominion. Lord, may I be obedient to what you will show me. Today, I am meeting with _____ so grant me encouraging words; I need to make a decision on _____ so grant me wisdom to know what to do; I need help in _____ so enable me to work diligently; and give me peace about _____. Lord, **"Your will be done, on earth as it is in heaven,"** and I fully submit to your plans instead of mine. May I do the best that I can but leave the outcome to you and not demand my own way. Daddy, **"Give us today our daily bread,"** for we are financially lacking to pay for our _____. Lord, thank you for caring for my needs. Father, please **"forgive us (me) our (my) debts (sins)."** I have sinned today, please forgive me for _____. Please help me live free from sin! I can't do this by myself! I desperately need your help. And, Lord, please help me to **"forgive our (my) debtors"** who hurt me. Help me to forgive them, and let my anger and bitterness toward _____ be removed. Dear God, **"lead me away from temp-**

tation" in _____ and help me to overcome _____. Moreover, **"deliver us (me) from the evil one,"** for I fear you and no other, not even the devil, for he is under your dominion. May you rule supremely over my life, for you are my Savior and the Master of my heart. May your Words be my shield and sword, and may your holy name give me strength for today. In Jesus name I pray, amen.

Remember, this is just a sample. Don't make this a ritual you read every day. Change it up. Break the routine. Speak honestly from your heart and enjoy His presence.

# -Chapter 12-

## Growing in Prayer

Once you have familiarized yourself with the Lord's Prayer and have become comfortable applying it on a daily basis, learning about other ways of praying will break the routine. Believe it or not; it is easy to get into a rut praying if you let it. Consistently seeking God through prayer is a spiritual battle, one that can easily be lost if every effort isn't made to win it. Prayer is so powerful; we dare not miss out on the medium God has provided for drawing us closer to Himself. The fact that He has included us in His plans is amazing, and His plans for our lives are communicated in prayer.

### James 5:13-16

13 Is anyone among you in trouble? Let them *pray*. Is anyone happy? Let them sing songs of praise. 14 Is anyone among you sick? Let them call the elders of the church to *pray* over them and anoint them with oil in the name of the Lord. 15 And the *prayer* offered in faith will make the sick person well; the Lord will raise them up. If they have sinned, they will be forgiven. 16 Therefore confess your sins to each other and *pray* for each

other so that you may be healed. The *prayer* of a righteous person is powerful and effective.

Apostle Paul told the Colossians that he is constantly praying for their spiritual growth.

### Colossians 1:9-11

[9] For this reason, since the day we heard about you, we have not stopped *praying* for you. We continually ask God to fill you with the knowledge of his will through all the wisdom and understanding that the Spirit gives, [10] so that you may live a life worthy of the Lord and please him in every way: bearing fruit in every good work, growing in the knowledge of God, [11] being strengthened with all power according to his glorious might so that you may have great endurance and patience.

Here is an example of the ministry of intercession. Paul is praying for people he never met to grow in their relationship with God. The apostle Paul is petitioning God to fill the Colossians with "the knowledge of his will," so they will bear "fruit in every good work," "being strengthened with all power," and "have great endurance and patience." God wants this for every believer so if you would like to know how to pray for any believer, follow the way that Paul prayed for the Colossians. Three more of Paul's intercessory prayers are recorded in the books Philippians and Ephesians:

## Philippians 1:9-11

[9] And this is my prayer: that your love may abound more and more in knowledge and depth of insight, [10] so that you may be able to discern what is best and may be pure and blameless for the day of Christ, [11] filled with the fruit of righteousness that comes through Jesus Christ—to the glory and praise of God.

## Ephesians 1:15-19

[15] For this reason, ever since I heard about your faith in the Lord Jesus and your love for all God's people, [16] I have not stopped giving thanks for you, remembering you in my prayers. [17] I keep asking that the God of our Lord Jesus Christ, the glorious Father, may give you the Spirit of wisdom and revelation, so that you may know him better. [18] I pray that the eyes of your heart may be enlightened in order that you may know the hope to which he has called you, the riches of his glorious inheritance in his holy people, [19] and his incomparably great power for us who believe.

## Ephesians 3:14-19

[14] For this reason I kneel before the Father, [15] from whom every family in heaven and on earth derives its name. [16] I pray that out of his glorious riches he may strengthen you with power through his Spirit in your inner being, [17] so that Christ may dwell in your hearts through faith. And I pray that you, being rooted and established in love, [18] may have power, together

with all the Lord's holy people, to grasp how wide and long and high and deep is the love of Christ, [19] and to know this love that surpasses knowledge—that you may be filled to the measure of all the fullness of God.

As you can see Paul doesn't pray lightly. He prays that every believer reach his full potential, the fullness of God. If God answers this prayer, and He will, we will all become just like Jesus, in whom "the fullness of deity dwells in bodily form" (Colossians 2:9). Don't pray lite prayers like, "Lord bless him" because how are we to know if He did it. Be specific as possible so there is no doubt that God did it. This way the glory will go to Him. If I pray that God fill you with the knowledge of His will, I will know He has answered when you grow to be more like Jesus. The reason why Paul asks God to fill the Colossians "with the knowledge of his will through all the wisdom and understanding that the Spirit gives," is so that they "may live a life worthy of the Lord and please Him in every way: bearing fruit in every good work, growing in the knowledge of God." The proof of being filled with the will of God is a righteous life. When we pray, we're not trying to cover all the bases so if something happens, we can credit God with the result. Instead, we reason according to our knowledge of who God is so that our prayers are related to what He wants us to do. In this way the more we know God and pray according to His will, the more of our prayers get answered.

The reason why Jesus got all of His prayers answered is because He knew the Father's will perfectly.

We don't just pray to get God to do something. Is a favor or a task the only reason you talk to your friends or family members? Paul told the Ephesian believers, "And pray in the Spirit on all occasions with all kinds of prayers and requests. With this in mind, be alert and always keep on praying for all the Lord's people" (Ephesians 6:18). What do you talk about with your family and friends? Everything. What should you talk about with the Lord? Everything, especially strength for God's people. A very popular and practical way to communicate with the Lord is by praying through the acronym "A.C.T.S." As explained next the procedure will help you keep in mind the areas to address during prayer. You won't miss anything if you follow the guideline of A.C.T.S.

## A.C.T.S.

The acronym A.C.T.S. is a simple method to help new believers to pray: **A**doration, **C**onfession, **T**hanksgiving and **S**upplication. This model comes from Philippians 4:6.

### Philippians 4:6 (ESV)
⁶ Do not be anxious about anything, but in everything by prayer and supplication with thanksgiving let your requests be made known to God.

Whether we use A.C.T.S. or others such as P.R.A.Y. (Praise, Repentance, Appreciation, & Yearnings), all help to direct us to God. As you mature in prayer, you may decide not to use them because your relationship with the Lord will become more fluid and spontaneous. It will be more like real life. Until you get to that comfortable point, use these guidelines to keep you focused on Him.

**Adoration:** I (Joseph) remember when my daughter said to me her first word "daddy." I was thrilled that she would recognize me and honor me by saying "daddy." God is no different in that regard. God is deserving of our praise, and it pleases our Lord to hear us offer words of adoration. I encourage you to be very specific. Once you get familiar with the Bible, you can read aloud passages that honor and glorify Him or use specific phrases such as "Lord, you deserve all the praise, honor, and glory," "For the Lord is the great God, the great King above all gods (Psalm 95:3)."

**Confession:** Acknowledgment or the declaration of guilt directly to God through prayer clears the way for deeper fellowship with Him. If we knowingly withhold our confession, God is not going to respond. Why should He? God will not be manipulated. We can't fool Him. Simply say, "Lord, I have sinned against you, I have done _____," "God, this person has hurt me and I have held a grudge toward him for _____. Please help me to let it go, and enable me to forgive him." The objective is to be honest about our heart condition to an almighty God who knows us and desires to forgive us.

**Thanksgiving**: People experiencing times of difficulty, hardship, and trials find it difficult to be grateful. However, as a new believer in Christ you understand that your life is now completely different. You have everything to be thankful for. Your eternal destiny has been changed. You have an enduring relationship with the heavenly Father. You have His sovereign protection. When you die, no matter how difficult life may be now, you will spend eternity with Him. You'll have a brand new body that doesn't age, never tires, enjoys everything, and lives forever. Comparatively speaking, even if we lived a thousand years full of pain and suffering, next to eternity, that would still be nothing. Any finite number divided by infinity is still zero. Tell God, "Thank you for forgiving me and loving me in spite of my sinfulness," "Though, I cannot walk, I thank you for this wheelchair that you provided." It was so encouraging to hear a man born blind say, "The first thing I will ever see is the Lord when I get to heaven." Not many people can say that. That believer was rejoicing over his blindness, and thankful for the reality of his future with the Lord. With that kind of attitude, I'm sure his present relationship with the Lord is filled with joy and contentment.

**Supplication:** This part of the prayer model is to make requests to the almighty God. But it doesn't begin until after you have given God adoration, confession of your sins, and expression of gratitude. Make a request such as "God, please help with _____." But be willing to give the request to God so He can bring about the outcome He desires. This is an important principle to follow. Jesus Himself said, "May Your will be done," knowing that He would die the next day (Matthew 26:42). Jesus entrusted the outcome of His life to His sovereign Father. Even though Jesus experienced an excruciating death, He redeemed you and me. Jesus had in mind His own comfort but submitted to the Father's will. The result was infinitely better. Had Jesus not gone to the cross, we wouldn't be writing this book right now and you and I would still be living in sin. Praise Jesus for submitting to the Father's will.

To close go back to "Adoration." Praise Him once again before saying, "Amen." He is deserving.

## When and How Long to Pray

I am convinced prayer is the determining factor between mild stirrings and deep breakthroughs in life. The difference between mediocrity and greatness is measured by your prayer life. The more we pray the more God works. Jesus demonstrated that prayer was His secret source of spiritual strength and the reservoir of real refreshment. Even when he was very busy, he was never too busy to pray. Prayer was the first of Jesus' daily activities and appointments and the first item on his calendar (Mark 1:35).

Though you can pray anywhere at any time on any day, it is best to set a consistent time each day. Begin by setting a time either at night or early morning Monday through Sunday. Start with fifteen to thirty minutes of prayer time, including Scripture reading.

I (Joseph) operated my own business for many years and used this opportunity to go into my office early to pray and read my Bible. After a solid time of prayer and the Word, I would turn the sign to "open" for business. Those vital moments with the Lord gave me discernment and wisdom in business matters, helping me to successfully grow the business as I applied Christian principles.

## Consistent Place to Pray

Going to my office early and on a daily basis prepared my mind to meet with the Lord. I could communicate with the Lord without any distractions. If Jesus had a favorite place to pray during His earthly life, the Mount of Olives was certainly one of them. Inside the Mount of Olives was a garden called Gethsemane which means "the garden of the oil press." Jesus often went there to pray, and it was there He was found praying when they arrested Him before His crucifixion.

For Moses the place to commune with the Lord was the Tent of Meeting. This particular tent was made sacred because of the divine dialogue that went on inside between Moses and God. When Moses went inside, distractions were minimized, and it made the meeting time with the Lord a very special occasion. Moses would come out refreshed and renewed, ready to handle the stresses of the day. His time with the Lord prepared him to deal with complicated situations and difficult relational issues.

### Exodus 33:7-11

[7] Now Moses used to take a tent and pitch it outside the camp some distance away, calling it the "tent of meeting." Anyone inquiring of the LORD would go to the tent of meeting outside the camp. [8] And whenever Moses went out to the tent, all the people rose and stood at the entrances to their tents, watching Moses until he entered the tent. [9] As Moses went into the tent, the pillar of cloud would come down and stay at the entrance, while the LORD spoke with Moses. [10] Whenever the people saw the pillar of cloud standing at the entrance to the tent, they all stood and worshiped, each at the entrance to their tent. [11] The LORD would speak to Moses face to face, as one speaks to a friend.

# Journaling

During prayer, I would make petitions and ask questions, often receiving answers directly from reading His Word. As I received answers from the Scriptures, I would write them down and reflect on them. The more I meditated upon the answers, the clearer it became. The clarity helped me make the right decision in what I was contemplating. Spending time with the Lord was amazing every time. God would bring a thought to mind or reveal an insight through His Word which I would write down. When the messages were not clear, I would pray daily until the Lord gave me clarity. At every crucial decision point of my life, I noticed in my journal that God had not only answered my prayers, but showed me better paths to choose.

We're all busy, so why add another activity to my schedule you ask? Plain and simple, journaling helps you remember the goodness of God. If we don't journal, we might forget what God brought to our minds. If He gives direction, speaks to our hearts, or convicts us of something important, shouldn't we remember them? When God gives us a special dream or a unique vision, journaling will help us not to forget it. Years later, when it gets fulfilled, you can actually trace it back to its origins and remind yourself of the goodness of our great God. During my time of trials and difficulties, I have often looked back on my journal to remind myself of how God had always shown up and prevailed in my situations. He has never let go of His love for me and my family. Let me encourage you to try journaling for 30 days, and if you see the benefits, continue it for one year. After a year, re-evaluate. I predict you won't be able to stop, but it's strictly up to you.

# Part 4

# Spiritual

# Growth

I f someone asks you, "How have you spiritually grown over the past year?" what would you say? If you just became a Christian last week, you wouldn't know how to answer except to say, "I just began my spiritual life a week ago." But if you picked this book up to learn how to grow spiritually even though you became a Christian some time ago, you may already

# 4

# Spiritual

# Growth

have an idea of what spiritual growth is. Just to be safe and clear we'll let God's word define for us what spiritual growth means. According to Romans 8:29 "For those God foreknew he also predestined to be conformed to the image of his Son." This means that spiritual growth is determined by how much we are "conforming to the image" of Christ. Whether it is in our actions, words, or thoughts, we haven't grown if we are not more like Christ today than we were a week ago.

Not to be confused with spiritual maturity, spiritual growth is the progression of the individual toward the character of Christ. Spiritual maturity is the attainment of a certain level of growth. Think about a child. He may be growing but not mature. For people maturity is self-control, responsibility for one's actions, the ability to take care of others, and a certain level of wisdom and knowledge. It's the same way spiritually speaking. A person may be growing spiritually, but not spiritually mature. A Christian is spiritually mature when he is able to distinguish good from evil and practice the good. A Christian is mature because his faith is grounded in the truths of God's Word and his actions reflect his commitment to it. He is not persuaded to deviate from what is right.

### Hebrews 5:14

But solid food is for the **mature**, who by constant use have trained themselves to distinguish good from evil.

A Christian is growing when he is learning more about God's character, is able to practice the spiritual disciplines of prayer, Bible study, evangelism, and service, and reflecting the character of God in an increasing way. Now let us look at the factors that contribute to our spiritual growth in the following few chapters.

# -Chapter 13-

## Obedience

The primary focus in your effort to live the Christian life should be obedience. Obedience is how you became a Christian, and it is the way you grow. Nobody grows without it. To love the Lord your God with all your heart, and with all your soul, and with all your mind, and with all your strength is a command (Deuteronomy 6:5; Matthew 22:37; Mark 12:30; Luke 10:27). In order to follow that command, you must obey God in everything.

When you became a Christian you obeyed the command "Believe in the Lord Jesus and you shall be saved" (Acts 16:31). If at all possible a second command that needs to be obeyed is the command to be baptized. So if you haven't been baptized, make arrangements to be baptized. Ask the one who led you to the Lord or a mature Christian or a leader in a church to baptize you. You don't need a lengthy doctrinal seminar to understand the command to be baptized. Simply put: Baptism is an outward demonstration of an inward reality. It is a public declaration that you have given your life to the Lord to follow Him for the rest of your life, and you want everyone to know it, not because you want to boast that somehow you have a new prestigious position, but that you are declaring a new loyalty and life. You are celebrating the reality that you have been transferred from the kingdom of darkness to God's glorious kingdom of light. Isn't that worth celebrating? Let's look at two examples.

The book of Acts records Peter preaching his first sermon after the resurrection and ascension of Jesus. Three thousand were saved and were baptized immediately as a sequel to conversion. Baptism was included in the gospel message when Peter said, "'Repent and be baptized, every one of you, in the name of Jesus Christ for the forgiveness of your sins. And you will receive the gift of the Holy Spirit'" (Acts 2:38). When the people who heard his message believed, they were baptized. "Those who accepted his message were baptized, and about three thousand were added to their number *that day*" (Acts 2:41).

When the Ethiopian eunuch in Acts 8:26-38 was saved, he wanted to be baptized right then. Even though there is no recorded mention of baptism in these verses, we know that it was part of the gospel presentation by Philip because the eunuch asked Philip to baptize him as soon as they approached water. The verse reads, "As they traveled along the road, they came to some water and the eunuch said, 'Look, here is water. Why shouldn't I be baptized?' And he gave orders to stop the chariot. Then both Philip and the eunuch went down into the water and Philip baptized him" (Acts 8:36-38).

You see in both cases that a sign of conversion was the willingness to be obedient in the act of baptism after believing the gospel. There was no hesitation or reluctance on the part of those who were converted. They were glad to participate in the symbolism. Right after believing they wanted to publically declare their new-found faith and loyalty in the Lord Jesus. For additional examples read about Cornelius and his family (Acts 10:1-48) and the jail guard and his family (Acts 16:16-34).

If you haven't been baptized yet, make arrangements with a church leader or the one who shared with you the gospel to get baptized. A pool, a river, the beach, or a baptismal of a church can be used as a place for baptism. During the war with Iraq, the soldiers who got converted were baptized in a hole dug for the purpose with a plastic lining to keep the water from being absorbed into the ground. They got baptized in the middle of the desert during a war. If there is a will, there is a creative way to get it done. Consult with your church leader for further guidance in this matter.

---

**Short Answer**: Primary Point of Obedience

Have you ever wondered why Jesus did what He did? Jesus knew that betrayal would come from His disciples. He was willing to face the harsh persecution from the Jewish leaders.

**Continuation:**

He knew He would endure physical torture, but instead of pulling the plug, He went through it. Why? OBEDIENCE. Obedience is the supreme test of faith in God (1 Samuel 28:18).

Jesus obeyed God the Father so that the sins of the world could fall on Him. He went forward because that was the goal set by God in order to reconcile man to God. Jesus completed the task because it was His divine appointment. The plan was executed to perfection because Jesus walked the path that was set for Him. And, because Jesus obeyed God's will, we now have freedom from sin's eternal condemnation and can live in the abundance of his grace.

## Understanding the Need for Obedience

Now let's lay the groundwork for the necessity of obedience when anyone becomes a Christian. To fully appreciate the critical nature of this theme we must travel back in time to the Garden of Eden. According to Genesis 2:16-17, Adam was specifically and emphatically commanded not to eat from the tree of the knowledge of good and evil. Eve was not yet created so Adam was the only one who received the command. Subsequent to the prohibition of eating from "the tree", God put Adam into a deep sleep and cloned another human being out of his rib. Fortunately for Adam it turned out to be a complement instead of a duplicate. Eve was born or, more accurately, created.

Shortly afterwards, the serpent is introduced as one who was "more crafty than any of the animals the Lord God made" (Genesis 3:1). And apparently he was free to roam throughout the earth however he pleased because he was in the garden too. From here on we must pay close attention to every minute detail of what went on between the serpent and the woman.

For a strategic reason which will be made clear later, the serpent approaches Eve instead of Adam. And instead of small talk, the serpent poses a direct question to Eve, challenging her knowledge of what went on between her husband and the Lord. "'Did God really say, 'You (*plural*) must not eat from any tree in the garden'?'" Now what makes this query so intriguing and cunning is the fact that Eve was not there when the command was given. So the only way she could have known what was said was what Adam told her. The serpent was testing whether there was good communication between the husband and the wife. In other words "Did God say this or did your husband say it?" Eve doesn't flinch. *"We may eat fruit from the trees in the garden, but God did say, 'You must not eat fruit from the tree that is in the middle of the garden, and you must not touch it, or you will die,'"* (Gen 3:2-3) was her reply.

There are at least three problems with her response. First of all she tells the serpent that "we" may eat fruit from the trees in the garden when she wasn't told not to eat it. Only Adam was told not to eat from it. If her husband told her not to, then the blame would be on him, and if she assumed she couldn't eat from it because Adam told her *he* couldn't, than the blame would be on her. At this point we do not know if there was a breakdown in communication or if an assumption was made.

The second problem with her recall of what God said is she leaves out a word "free" in NIV and "freely" in KJV, and the difference between "We may eat" and "We may freely eat" can be an eternity. While Eve is emphasizing the casual nature of the liberty, God was focusing on what a blessing it was to have so much. You may recall when He made the garden, *"...the Lord God made all kinds of trees grow out of the ground — trees that were pleasing to the eye and good for food"* (Genesis 2:9). It wasn't a matter of the glass being half empty or half full; rather, while God was highlighting the glass as 99.9% full, she was looking at the 0.1% that was empty. If we got so busy doing what God wanted us to do, we wouldn't have time to run into the things God doesn't want us to do. We would avoid the negatives simply by doing the positives.

The third problem with Eve's answer to the serpent's question was that she added to what God said. God never said anything about not touching the tree. His only prohibition was not to eat the fruit. They could have built a tree-house on it. Adam could have picked the fruits and juggled them, and they could have thrown some rotten ones at each other. She could have decorated her house with them. But the fruit was not to be eaten. So how does the serpent exploit her weakness?

The serpent comes back with a direct contradiction of what God said. *"You will not surely die,"* the serpent said to the woman. *"For God knows that when you eat of it your eyes will be opened, and you will be like God, knowing good and evil"* (Genesis 3:4-5). Cunning is an understatement. Look at his approach. First of all "You" is plural meaning you and your husband. Both Adam and Eve will not die and both will know good and evil if they eat the fruit, the serpent says. Remember, only Adam was prohibited from eating the fruit not Eve. Look how bold he is when talking about the word of God. A direct contradiction doesn't even faze him. He can lie with a straight face and with depraved confidence. He even declares that it is God's fault that Adam and Eve don't have the knowledge of good and evil. "God knows" and He is the one keeping this good thing from you. You deserve it, and you should have it. What's stopping you when it is in your power to have it? This is the serpent's line of reasoning. And Eve falls for it. Eve had three good reasons for eating the fruit: the tree was edible, the fruit looked good, and it would make her wise as she understood it.

Now careful attention needs to be paid to the sequence of events that took place from here on. *"6 When the woman saw that the fruit of the tree was good for food and pleasing to the eye, and also desirable for gaining wisdom, she took some and ate it. She also gave some to her husband, who was with her, and he ate it. 7 Then the eyes of both of them were opened, and they realized they were naked; so they sewed fig leaves together and made coverings for themselves"* (Gen 3:6-7).

The question that must be asked is this? What happened to Eve when she ate the fruit? The answer from Scripture is nothing. She ate first and nothing happened. She gave some to her husband, and after he ate the eyes of both of them were opened. The reason why this is so important is this: Adam was given the command not to eat from the tree not Eve. When she ate nothing happened to her because God didn't command her not to eat from it. The reason the Scripture says that Eve was deceived (Gen 3:13) is because the serpent lied to her about gaining wisdom and her eyes being opened if she ate. If the serpent were telling the truth it would have happened this way. Eve would have eaten the fruit and her eyes would have been opened so she would have told Adam that they were naked. She would have covered herself up and would have tried to cover Adam up. He would have been perplexed as to why Eve was acting so abnormally. She would have told Adam to not eat the fruit because of the consequences. Instead, since Eve felt nothing and nothing happened, she could confidently give some to her husband to find out if anything would happen to him. When he ate, the consequence came upon both of them and sent the rippling effects down to their posterity. Everyone after Adam experienced the curse of his disobedience through his DNA. It was Adam who disobeyed God and Eve who encouraged him to do so.

Because of Adam's disobedience, we experience all kinds of pain and suffering. The sinful nature we inherited from Adam drives us away from God and makes us His enemies. The consequences of disobedience are listed in Genesis 3 and Deuteronomy 28 among others. It is for this reason the Lord Jesus came into the world. Disobedience was the problem and Jesus was the solution-Genesis 3:15. Jesus would eventually "crush" Satan's head because he was ultimately the cause of the disobedience. As a matter of fact the Greatest Commission of Matthew 28:19-20 is a call to obedience.

[19] *Therefore go and make disciples of all nations, baptizing them in the name of the Father and of the Son and of the Holy Spirit,* [20] *and teaching them to obey everything I have commanded you. And surely I am with you always, to the very end of the age."*

As matter of fact the entire Bible can be summed up as a division of disobedience and obedience. How? The first 3 chapters of Genesis describe the background and act of disobedience and the rest of the Bible is God's solution to bring about ob-

153

edience. It cannot be understated that OBEDIENCE is the calling for all mankind, especially the believers.

## John 14:15

[15] "If you love me, keep my commands.

## Romans 2:13

[13] For it is not those who hear the law who are righteous in God's sight, but it is those who obey the law who will be declared righteous.

## 2 Corinthians 10:5

[5] We demolish arguments and every pretension that sets itself up against the knowledge of God, and we take captive every thought to make it obedient to Christ.

# -Chapter 14-

## Discipleship/Mentorship

Of course we can spiritually grow on our own. We can study the Bible, pray, serve people inside and outside the church, and share our faith. These are the means by which we grow. But two areas that are crucial for our maturity in the faith when neglected can have a detrimental impact on our walk with the Lord and lead us into all kinds of error and sin. These are discipleship (and his older brother mentorship) and fellowship.

## Discipleship

Discipleship is like a teacher-student relationship where the discipler does most of the guiding and holds the agenda. But more than a teacher-student relationship, at its core discipleship is the transfer of the lifestyle and character of the discipler to the disciple. More often than not the discipler is the initiator and seeks to train another believer into the character of Christ. The process goes on until the disciple becomes just like his discipler and is usually short term, about 1-3 years, meeting frequently. Activities include doing ministry together, studying the Word together, and delving deeply into each others' lives.

A very strong bond occurs through the relationship and they become lifelong friends. After becoming a believer in college, I (Jae) used to meet with my discipler, every week for prayer and accountability for about 2 years, and since we lived together, there weren't very many areas of our lives we didn't share together or didn't know about each other. I learned how to pray like he did, I learned to study the Bible like he did, I learned how to do evangelism like he did, and I learned what it meant to be a godly college student like he was. Through the process I grew very fast in the Lord and eventually became a leader in 2 years and in 3 years had my own ministry. And as you will see in the description of mentorship, in most cases mentorship is born out of discipleship although it's not the only way that mentorship occurs.

## Mentorship

Mentorship is a form of discipleship, but because there are some differences, I will make the distinction here. Mentorship is normally initiated by the mentee to learn about a specific area or areas of his life that he would like to improve with the help of the mentor. Although the time commitment (frequency) is much less than discipleship, people in mentorship have a longer relationship because they meet or talk together over a longer period of time. Mentorship focuses not on frequency but on the subject of interest. Whereas discipleship is the building of the character, mentorship assumes that for the most part and seeks to gain perspective, understanding, and insight. Derek, my mentor, taught me what a leader was, what the end times was going to look like, what was wrong with pre-nuptials, and what role hardships played in my spiritual growth, just to mention a few. It is not that character can't be addressed in mentorship; it is limited since lives are not spent together to have that kind of accountability. Although my roommate Dave was my discipler, he was not the one who led me to the Lord. Derek did. But because Derek and I couldn't meet as often, he became my mentor. I consulted him as often as I could, and we got together whenever we had the opportunity. We still get together to talk, and I seek his wisdom whenever I need perspective or insight on a particular matter.

After college Dave also became my mentor, and I've also been in mentorship with him over the past 20 years. What began as discipleship became mentorship because our friendship continued. It was interesting to realize that it is still Dave who helps with the doing aspects of my life and Derek who helps me with the thinking aspects of my life. I learned from Dave how to homeschool my children, hold a leadership training weekend, and find the area of ministry in keeping with God's giftedness to me, among other things. On the other hand, it was Derek who shared with me his understanding of Scriptures through 2-3 decades of study. I got my definition of leadership from him. I know why suffering needs to be embraced because of his teaching. He helped me think through Scriptures.

## Finding a Mentor

With the understanding of discipleship and mentorship in mind, it is time to find someone who will do that for you. Pray that God will provide. You never know whom God will send to guide you on your way toward maturity in Christ. You should also ask God about approaching someone to be a discipler or mentor. Once you find a church and the pastor who leads it, he will automatically become a mentor to you. Since he is available for consultation and guidance, the mentorship relationship begins with your first call to him. As you participate in the local church, you will also notice individuals who set good examples that attract you.

The kinship you feel with another believer is one way the Lord will use to bring you two together. Also, in answer to your prayer the Lord may send you someone who will ask if you would like to join his ministry with the opportunity to grow personally in your walk with the Lord through his leadership. Be open to such opportunities, always with the understanding that you need to exercise wisdom in accepting or foregoing them. In my experience until a baby believer reaches a certain level of maturity, God provides very timely, specific, and clear guidance that will help him grow. Let me illustrate: I didn't even know to look for a discipler because I didn't know what one was. All I knew when I became a Christian was that I loved the Lord and I wanted to read His Word and pray. My high school friend Joe, who was also at Drexel University with me, asked if I wanted to be his roommate along with 2 others. I jumped at the chance to live with 3 believers who were further along in their walk with my newfound Lord. Joe didn't ask me earlier because the rule at the "friendly apartments" was that only believers could be invited- the justification being spiritual battles were reserved for outside the home instead of inside. I said, "Yes," knowing that one of his roommates was Dave who happened to be the Intervarsity Christian Fellowship president. My desire was to learn a lot from just living with the brother. Shortly after my moving in, Dave asked me to meet with him as prayer partner. It was God's provision to me as a young believer needing a discipler.

How did the relationship change after we graduated from college? Dave moved to North Carolina, and I moved back to Maryland so we couldn't meet as often as we used to. But we did keep in touch and our discipleship relationship turned into mentorship as most discipleship relationships do. To use the analogy of the family: the father disciples the son to be a godly man and afterwards becomes his advisor or mentor for life; the same goes for the mother-daughter relationship. The impact that he had on my life can't be forgotten. The longing in the heart of the disciple is to maintain the fellowship that he enjoyed with his discipler. Not only that but the discipler loves the disciple, so there is desire on both sides to maintain the relationship. The natural overflow of the discipleship relationship is to convert it to mentorship. It's usually for life.

**Short Answers**: Discipleship and Mentorship

**Discipleship**: Would you rather read about cooking or have someone show you step by step? This is what a discipler does with his disciple. He teaches and shows the disciple how to be more like Christ in character and mindset. It is an intense process because there are tough times of character development. But the reward is a faster growth toward maturity.

This is not a forced relationship. Like a soldier who enlists and puts himself through the rigors of boot camp and war simulations, a disciple voluntarily summits to one who is more mature in order to learn from him. "Whoever wants to be my disciple must deny himself and take up his cross and follow me" (Matthew 16:24).

**Continuation**:

**Mentorship**: A mentor advises on the specific needs of the mentee. Mentorship is less about character development and more about perspective because the mentee has achieved a level of character and maturity. In most cases mentorship is born out of discipleship, but not the other way around.

In a family the father is a discipler to his sons and later becomes a mentor when his sons become adults. Seek a discipler when you are young in the faith. As you get older and more mature, multiple mentors will be more helpful for gaining perspective. Ask the Lord to provide you a discipler or mentors. You will grow so much through them.

The Bible has many examples of mentoring relationships; Barnabas and Saul, Paul and Timothy, and Jesus and the Disciples to just mention a few about great mentors of the Bible. The one that strikes me the most is a mentor to one of the most powerful and influential Hebrew leader.

Here is Jethro, the priest of Midian and father-in-law to Moses who "heard of everything God had done for Moses and for his people Israel, and how the Lord had brought Israel out of Egypt" (Exodus 18:1). Moses had shown great leadership in guiding his people from the hands of the mighty Pharaoh. Yet it was Jethro who helped the celebrated leader of the Israelites become the great leader as the judge. Mentorship works and God will call upon His children to guide and counsel those He calls to faith.

## Exodus 18:13-23

[17]Moses' father-in-law said to him, "What you are doing is not good. [18]You and the people with you will certainly wear yourselves out, for the thing is too heavy for you. You are not able to do it alone. [19]Now obey my voice; I will give you advice, and God be with you! You shall represent the people before God and bring their cases to God, [20]and you shall warn them about the statutes and the laws, and make them know the way in which they must walk and what they must do. [21]Moreover, look for able men from all the people, men who fear God, who are trustworthy and hate a bribe, and place such men over the people as chiefs of thousands, of hundreds, of fifties, and of tens. [22]And let them judge the people at all times. Every great matter they shall bring to you, but any small matter they shall decide themselves. So it will be easier for you, and they will bear the burden with you. [23]If you do this, God will direct you, you will be able to endure, and all this people also will go to their place in peace."

# -Chapter 15-

## Fellowship

Now let us look at the second crucial area of our need toward maturity: fellowship. Fellowship is the interaction with brothers and sisters in the Lord in a group setting that gives us the opportunity to practice building up and encouraging of one another. Notice that this is a mutual effort. If it is only one-sided, it is called teaching, mentorship, or discipleship. Fellowship happens as everyone in the group intentionally centers the interaction on strengthening one another in the Lord. In the second chapter of Acts this was an obvious need as the new believers didn't know much but were facing persecution from the world. How were they to be strengthened to continue in their walk with the Lord as mere babes in Christ? When the three thousand got saved, they gravitated toward several things that propelled them toward spiritual maturity.

### Acts 2:42-47

[42] They devoted themselves to the apostles' teaching and to fellowship, to the breaking of bread and to prayer. [43] Everyone was filled with awe at the many wonders and signs performed by the apostles. [44] All the believers were together and had eve-

rything in common. [45] They sold property and possessions to give to anyone who had need. [46] Every day they continued to meet together in the temple courts. They broke bread in their homes and ate together with glad and sincere hearts, [47] praising God and enjoying the favor of all the people. And the Lord added to their number daily those who were being saved.

Notice right after they got saved, they devoted themselves to solid teaching and *fellowship*. We've been talking about the necessity of God's Word at the outset of this book for good reason. We can't live without every Word that comes from the mouth of God. But we can't grow and live without fellowship either. More often than not we will lose zeal without encouragement. We will lose motivation to keep obeying God without encouragement. We will weary in doing good without encouragement. We will keep our faith only to ourselves if we don't have one another to motivate us to keep sharing it.

Look what is included in fellowship: prayer, praise, communion, sharing property, time spent together mingling, talking, and eating and all the while sharing their faith. Just getting together to say a prayer before eating is not fellowship. Feeling good about one another and enjoying each other's company is not fellowship. Doing them in church is not fellowship. Talking about sports, stocks, politics, work, homeschooling, internet activities, vacation choices and locations, classes, exams, girlfriends or boyfriends, TV shows and movies (ad nauseam) is not fellowship if they are done without God's perspective or for the purpose of doing them as the Lord's servant. Non-believers do it all the time. They don't have biblical fellowship. They call that partying and add alcohol to it. Fellowship is interacting with one another for the purpose of encouraging one another to keep walking with the Lord and maturing toward Christ-likeness. Fellowship is helping one another stay motivated to live the Christian life. Fellowship centers on God, His perspective, and His agenda. Here is how to have fellowship.

**Short Answers**: Christian Fellowship

**Fellowship**: Christian fellowship involves getting together with other believers for spiritual purposes: for sharing needs, prayer, edification in the Word, encouragement, comfort, and worship.

**1 John 1:7**

7 But if we walk in the light, as he is in the light, we have fellowship with one another, and the blood of Jesus, his Son, purifies us from all sin.

When you get together with other believers, ask one or more of these questions to keep the gathering focused on fellowship:

1. How did you become a Christian?
2. What is the Lord doing in your life right now?
3. What has the Lord taught you recently or what is He teaching you now?
4. How can I pray for you in your relationship with the Lord?
5. What is one issue you are dealing with spiritually that I can pray for?

Or

6. Start by saying, "I am in need of some perspective," and then share your spiritual struggle so that people may have the opportunity to share their feedback and pray for you.
7. Sing and worship the Lord together.
8. Break bread together.

After the activity this is how you know you've had fellowship. Answer these questions:

1. Did I encourage someone in the Lord?
2. Did someone encourage me in the Lord?
3. Am I more motivated to serve or seek the Lord now because of the interaction?
4. Was Christ the center of the interaction?

If the answer was yes to at least one of these questions, you had fellowship. If the answer was no to all these questions, fellowship didn't take place. For new believers we encourage you to have fellowship at least twice a week. The ideal is 3 or more times a week. Daily would be fantastic but not so realistic. Example: snacking or having lunch after service with a group of believers counts as 1, mid-week Bible study counts as 2, lunch with other believers during the week counts as the third. As a new believer I had fellowship every day because I lived with 3 Christians. We were always talking about the Lord because I asked questions all the time. I was the trigger in most cases because I was new. You will find that sometimes it is very difficult to keep focused on fellowship. Seasoned Christians need to stay alert because as their lives get busier, they can "grow out of" fellowship. Don't let this happen. Ask yourself every time you get together with other Christians, "Is this fellowship?" If it's not, make it so.

### 1 John 1:3

[3] We proclaim to you what we have seen and heard, so that you also may have fellowship with us. And our fellowship is with the Father and with his Son, Jesus Christ.

### Psalm 55:14

[14] with whom I once enjoyed sweet fellowship
at the house of God,

as we walked about
among the worshipers.

**Psalm 133:1**

[1] How good and pleasant it is
when God's people live together in unity!

# Breaking Bread

The greatest form of fellowship we can have with other believers is Holy Communion or breaking bread. While baptism
demonstrates to the unbelieving world that we have been
converted, breaking bread shows how we as a believing
community are remembering what the Lord did for us as we
wait for His return. Baptism only occurs once, but "communion" happens regularly. Breaking bread is only for believers
so participate in the commemoration whenever your church
offers it. Breaking bread is a formal reminder that we are
grateful for the Lord's redeeming work and that He will return to take us with Him to heaven. While remembering the
Lord's sacrifice, we are celebrating our freedom from the penalty of sin and rejoicing over our union with Him.

# Part 5

# Knowing God's Will

A question every Christian asks is "How do I know God's will for my life?" My natural response has been to say, "Do you know God's written will for your life?" Majority of the time, people will respond "No," or ask, "What do you mean by that?" Then, my next question has been to ask them if they have been reading their Bible on a

# 5

# Knowing

# God's

# Will

daily basis. Unfortunately, most believers do not read their Bibles daily nor pray on a consistent basis. I've been quick to encourage people to read and understand what God has already revealed through His Word. If you do not read God's Word, how can you claim you are interested in His will? If you don't pray, how can you claim you are interested in a relationship with your Savior? If you want to know God's will, you must know His heart, and His heart is revealed in His Word. You must know His heart to be able to determine His will. As you establish an intimate relationship with the Lord, He will guide you through prayer, His Word, others (including unbelievers), and circumstances.

**Psalm 119:105-106**

[105] Your word is a lamp for my feet,

a light on my path.

[106] I have taken an oath and confirmed it,

that I will follow your righteous laws.

First and foremost, in order to "hear from God" you must have a relationship with Him. And since you began that relationship a short time ago, you qualify to hear Him speak to you personally. He has a plan for you to reach the top of your potential:

**Jeremiah 29:11**

[11] For I know the plans I have for you," declares the LORD, "plans to prosper you and not to harm you, plans to give you hope and a future.

For many Christians, one of the most complex and elusive things they encounter is determining the will of God for their life. Some seem to know the road God would have them journey, but hesitate to follow it while small minorities of others quickly determine the will of God for them and immediately follow it. Because of the complexity of knowing God's will, the following chapters will help you understand the will of God for your life through prayer, His Word, Christian service and wise counsel.

## **Short Answers**: Knowing God's Will

**Step 1**: Pray and God will remind you of His Word and speak to your heart. [For details on prayer, go to Part 3.]

**Step 2**: Read His Word and you will know His heart.

**Step 3**: Start serving at your home church and get equipped to fulfill the Great Commission (Read Matthew 28:18-20). As you serve, you'll be challenged to grow. He'll stretch you. Make sure to read chapter 18 "Knowing God's Will through Christian Service."

**Step 4**: Seek wise counsel from mature Christians before making big decisions. God may speak through them and give you a message of wisdom or discernment, chapter 19.

**Step 5**: Wait patiently, pray, stay in the Word, and the Lord will give you confirmation, conviction, and peace in your heart.

# Chapter 16

# Knowing God's Will through Prayer

It was the middle of December when I (Jae) finished my fall quarter, I still had no job for my winter and spring quarters which was supposed to begin the first week of January. During my work-study program half of the school year was to be spent doing work in my major, electrical engineering, while the other half was to be spent on academics. With only three weeks to look for a job, I was home in Baltimore when I should have been in Philadelphia interviewing. Desperate for an answer and feeling the pressure of my unbelieving family's critical eye, I earnestly prayed for a job. But rather than addressing my joblessness, the Lord was pointing to my disconnectedness with my family. We were in tension because back in November I had turned down a job offer in Baltimore to look for one in Philly. They didn't understand living by faith. They wondered why I was so unwise as to not take a job offer in Baltimore when I was not guaranteed a job in Philly. But I turned it down because I was convinced that the Lord wanted me to stay in Philly to work. That was the complaint from my family. They thought I was crazy for living by faith and brought this problem on myself.

As I prayed, the Lord guided me to reconcile with my family. He convinced me that my relationship with my family had to be right before I received my job. This was the conviction that I was receiving from the Lord during my prayers. So, I went to my mother and older sister and apologized for being inconsiderate. They were helping with my college tuition because my work-study earnings, along with grants and loans, weren't enough. If I didn't have a job because I was foolish or presumptuous, I would have been burdening them unnecessarily. I should have taken the sure thing instead of gambling with something uncertain-was my family's reasoning. I apologized for not informing them properly of my dilemma of being called to work in Philly rather than Baltimore. I convinced my mother and older sister that it would be better to work in Philly because I wouldn't have to move my stuff out of my apartment only to move it back six months later. I also predicted that I would be paid more in Philly. The Lord granted me favor in their eyes and our relationship was cleared. Somehow they agreed with my reasoning, but wondered how I would find a job in 3 weeks. My next prayer wasn't so profound: "Lord, now that my family relationship is cleared, all I need is the job."

What happened next I wouldn't have predicted in a million years, especially as a new believer of only 6 months. About an hour later I received a call from my work-study coordinator Mr. Severn. His job was to help students get matched up with companies for their work-study. Mr. Severn told me that he had the personnel manager of RCA on the other line, and all I need to tell him was my current GPA. When I told him it was 3.5, he told me to hang on for an answer. After talking with the personnel manager, Mr. Severn told me I had the job and could begin in the first week of January. He also informed me that I needed to come in the next day to fill out an application and deliver it to the personnel office as soon as possible. God was truly in charge. When was the last time someone got hired without an interview and before filling out an application? I learned a great lesson about finding God's will through prayer.

The priority goes to relationships. Before He answers prayer about personal needs, He mandates that we deal with our relationships that are not reconciled. Jesus commands in Matthew 5:24 to "leave your gift there in front of the altar. First go and be reconciled to them; then come and offer your gift." Furthermore, James 5:16 declares, "Therefore confess your sins to each other and pray for each other so that you may be healed. The prayer of a righteous person is powerful and effective." God tells us first to confess our sins to each other i.e. reconcile our relationships with each other before we ask for healing, a job, or any other need. And by the way when I received my acceptance letter from RCA, I was informed that I would receive a specific salary, which was 40% more than what I would have gotten at the Baltimore company. My family couldn't believe it. They didn't admit it, but they knew that the Lord showed Himself to be amazing. Praise the Lord.

## 1 John 5:14-15

[14] This is the confidence we have in approaching God: that if we ask anything according to his will, he hears us. [15] And if we know that he hears us—whatever we ask—we know that we have what we asked of him.

**Short Answers**: Knowing God's Will through Prayer

**Step 1**: Pray for a right relationship with God.

**Step 2**: Follow God's convictions. By the leading of the Holy Spirit, reconcile your relationships with others. Confess your sins to God and others. Ask Him to clear your conscious of sin.

**Step 2**: Simply ask God to give you wisdom to make right decisions. "If any of you lacks wisdom, you should ask God, who gives generously to all without finding fault, and it will be given to you" (James 1:5).

We don't need to have all the answers and have everything figured out before we go to God in prayer to ask for something. Just pray about everything. Seek His face. He will lead you. I didn't know how to pray about my job, but as I was praying the Lord led me. A submissive heart and an unwavering faith are all He's looking for. God does not demand that you act or pray maturely before He answers your prayers. He knows you just started your walk with Him so He will be patient with you. As a matter of fact His patience is superhuman. No one on earth is as patient as He is. He's not a pushover, but His lovingkindness is immeasurable. As you pray, listen for His guidance. He will speak to you.

## God Answers

God will answer our prayers that are in agreement with His will. His answers are not always a yes, but are always in our best interest. When our desires line up with His will, we will come to understand how to pray so that we receive what we want, which is ultimately what He wants.

In order to find God's will through prayer, we must follow His principle, "ask and it will be given to you; seek and you will find; knock and the door will be opened to you" (Matthew 7:7). When we continue to ask, seek, and knock, God will respond, not because we wore Him out but because we let Him know how committed we are to that cause and because we believe He feels the same way. We show Him our greatest ambition in life is to fulfill His plan.

In 1 Samuel 1, we read of a woman named Hannah who was not able to bear a child. Her heart was broken, for she longed to be a mother. In desperation she prayed, "O Lord Almighty, if you will only look upon your servant's misery and remember me, and not forget your servant but give her a son" (1 Samuel 1:11). God answers in verse 19 and 20: "Early the next morning they arose and worshiped before the LORD and then went back to their home at Ramah. Elkanah made love to his wife Hannah, and the LORD remembered her. [20] So in the course of time Hannah became pregnant and gave birth to a son. She named him Samuel, saying, "Because I asked the LORD for him." Eventually, Samuel came to be the leading prophet for all Israel. He anointed the first two kings of Israel, Saul and David. Every year, Samuel used to go on a circuit judging for Israel among Ramah, Bethel, Gilgal and Mizpeh. God's will was to provide Israel with a prophet and when Hannah's prayer lined up with His, He granted her the request.

When I (Joseph) came back from Korea, I didn't bring home a Korean wife like my brothers. In the land of many beautiful women, I couldn't find one person to marry. My family was concerned since I was the only one out of six who wasn't married. My mother suggested that I should give God the opportunity to help me find a wife. "How was God going to help me find a wife?" I asked my mother in a pessimistic tone. She suggested that I pray and seek God's will for my future marriage. My mother had suggested these things before, but I never took it seriously because it didn't seem practical. With all my close friends married and my siblings all having children, I finally took my mother's suggestion seriously and decided to pray and seek God's will.

I took out a piece of paper and thought seriously about what I wanted in a woman. Would you believe that I actually wrote down 15 characteristics I wanted in a woman? With this list I started to pray almost every night about my future wife. When five months passed with no sign of an answer, I repented and apologized to God and shrunk the list to 10, thinking that I was asking too much. After seven months, I shrunk the list even further, to five. After ten months of prayer, I told God, "O.k. Lord! I understand. I still have too much, so may I just keep the first three and just stay focused on that?" Though I did pray only on the three, I eventually gave in and told God, "Not my will but your will be done." I remembered what Jesus did in Matthew 26:42, which was to give His will to God, "My Father, if it is not possible for this cup to be taken away unless I drink it, may your will be done." I decided to follow what Jesus did.

Some amazing things happened during that year. My married friends introduced to me some potential mates, but when things did not work out, I quickly moved on. This was unusual for me because my old self would not have given up. Instead, I learned to surrender to God and was at peace about not having my way. I would talk to God about these women, and His answers came in many different forms. For some, I didn't receive peace in my heart and for others there were no clarity in being married to them. And even though things didn't work out, I was convicted to keep trusting in Him.

Let me define peace, clarity, and conviction to make the points clear. Peace means there is nothing hindering or making me hesitate about the situation or decision. There is no uneasiness that I feel. For instance, if you decided to steal something, your conscience along with the Holy Spirit will stop you by telling you it's wrong. And if a decision is a bad one, your conscience will have nothing to say, but the Spirit of God who knows everything will make you uncomfortable as though you were doing something wrong (Psalm 139).

Clarity is a picture that comes up when we have a green light from God. We can see how it will work out. Yes, sometimes God gives us a negative picture for potentially wrong decisions, but more often than not, He just won't give us peace about the decision. When we can see things clearly, we will have peace. No picture came to mind when I thought about a life together with those women I was introduced to.

Conviction is any strong emotion that surfaces when thinking about a situation or decision. You may not know for sure why those emotions surface, but they will be strong.

When they come up, they need to be addressed because the Lord may be speaking to you through them. This is the Lord's way of telling us we need to investigate the matter.

Close to a year passed, and I was still focused on praying for a mate, with my short characteristics list in hand. Out of the blue, my old college friend called to ask if I would be interested in meeting a girl from his church. I said, "No," for three reasons. First, this girl lived seven states away. Second, my friend himself didn't have a girlfriend, so why would I trust his judgment. Third, when I asked how well he knew her, he told me that she was just an acquaintance. For two weeks straight, my friend persisted with his calls. I asked why he felt that we were right for each other. Even though his response wasn't clear, I trusted God to show me if this was it. I took a small vacation and drove to his house because he was going out of his way to do something considerate. I don't know many friends who would take time off from work and set up a four-day schedule to introduce me to a possible mate. The whole thing was very unusual.

When I first met my wife Jackie, I couldn't take my eyes off of her. Her personality, character, beauty, and love for God just overwhelmed me. God truly answered my prayer, but it was actually Jackie's prayer that God answered first. When Jackie prayed for a husband, God answered in minutes, but my prayer for a wife took close to a year. Her prayer was simple but direct. She asked God that her future husband would approach her and tell her his name was Joseph and that he was the youngest in his family, like the story of Joseph in the Bible. My mom named me Joseph even though I objected-I didn't want to be mistreated by my brothers like the Biblical Joseph. Apparently the Lord was leading both women on my behalf.

During the long distance relationship, both Jackie and I prayed continually for God's will in our relationship. God gave us clarity and peace about where we were headed. Further evidence that we were right for one another also came from wise and mature Christians, who confirmed there was nothing stopping us from getting married. It turns out that the Lord provided me a woman who had the 15 characteristics I was originally looking for. Through this experience, I learned three basic principles of understanding God's will through prayer:

1. **Pray consistently** to keep in touch with God. If you want God's guidance and the comfort of knowing He is walking with you, stay in tune with Him through prayer.

2. **Follow God's direction**, conviction, correction, and peace. Our ways are not always His ways, so following His ways is always best.

3. **Trust God** to do what's best for you. Leave the results to Him knowing that He is sovereign. If you are an-

xious or worried about an outcome, you are not trusting in His sovereignty. If you have peace no matter what the outcome, you have left the results up to Him.

Remember, when you pray **"Your will be done,"** you are asking the Father to have His way in you. You are surrendering your will in order to receive God's best for you. Ultimately, God's blue print becomes your blue print and His desires become your desires **"on earth, as it is in heaven."**

## Convictions during Prayer

As we seek God's will for our lives, we will be convicted to:

1. Forgive someone
2. Seek forgiveness and reconciliation
3. Break the bondage of sin
4. Break the bondages of guilt and shame
5. Take a step of Faith
6. Give with joy
7. Address other issues surfaced by the Holy Spirit

During prayer God will bring these issues to mind because He has a plan to move us forward in our spiritual growth. God will ask us to confess, repair, mend or simply break completely the things (sins, un-forgiveness, bitterness, etc.) that hold us from moving on.

When we come to the realization that we have done wrong, God wants us to quickly repent and confess to Him. He also commands us to admit to others we were wrong **"And forgive us our debts, as we also have forgiven our debtors."** When we don't seek reconciliation (whether we were right or wrong), lingering guilt results which can lead to spiritual bondage. The conviction in our hearts comes from the Holy Spirit, and God wants us to be wise about how we deal with sin and guilt. Remember, Satan does not want sin and guilt to leave you. He wants you to stay under a thick cloud of guilt so that your service to God is hindered. Don't get under the yoke of Satan's accusations. Devil means "slanderer" (1 Peter 5:8), and he never stops pointing his finger at God's children. He will tempt, accuse, lie, deceive, destroy, intimidate, and kill God's people if he can. Satan is constantly opposing God's agenda. That's why he's called the adversary of God.

Satan tries to tell us that forgiveness is never enough. He wants us to suffer for our sins. He's out to prove that we are not worthy of God's forgiveness. As a matter of fact, he is right. We are not worthy of forgiveness. That is why Christ had to die for us. Apart from Christ, we will never be worthy. So instead of feeling guilty about our unworthiness, be grateful. Praise God for providing a solution. Every time Satan accuses you of being unworthy, agree and thank God for forgiving you anyway. This way you use Satan's weapon against him. He will get tired of accusing you since his every accusation results in praise of God.

Know the difference between the conviction of the Holy Spirit and the condemnation of Satan. When the Holy Spirit speaks, he is specific about a particular sin. When Satan speaks, he is general about our sinfulness. Whenever he is specific about a sin, he's not interested in repentance but condemnation. Let me give some examples:

Let's say you used a four-letter word during a conversation. The Holy Spirit says, "That is an unwholesome word. Keep your mind pure and be a good example." Satan, however, says, "What a filthy mouth! You claim to be a Christian, and you're using profanity? You'll never change." Notice that Satan is not leading you toward repentance and therefore, away from God, but the Holy Spirit is specific about the change that needs to take place and with no condemnation. Romans 8:1 tell us "there is now no condemnation for those who are in Christ Jesus." God has removed the spiritual penalty of sin so our relationship with Him can never be changed. But we will face the consequences of our sin while on earth. If you sin by lying to your boss, you may lose your job, but you won't lose your salvation.

**Ephesians 6:10**

[10] Finally, be strong in the Lord and in his mighty power.

# Seeking God's Wisdom for Right Decisions

In 1 Kings 3 we learn that God appeared to a newly-appointed king named Solomon. In a dream the Lord propositioned Solomon, "Ask for whatever you want me to give you" (1 Kings 3:5). As a young king, Solomon could have asked for anything that his heart desired, yet seeing the magnitude of the responsibility he had as king, he asked for a "discerning heart" both to govern God's people and "to distinguish between right and wrong" (1 Kings 3:9). Because of Solomon's righteous motives, God gave Solomon what he asked for plus much more.

**1 Kings 3: 10 - 14**

[10] The Lord was pleased that Solomon had asked for this. [11] So God said to him, "Since you have asked for this and not for long life or wealth for yourself, nor have asked for the death of your enemies but for discernment in administering justice, [12] I will do what you have asked. I will give you a wise and discerning heart, so that there will never have been anyone like you, nor will there ever be. [13] Moreover, I will give you what you have not asked for—both wealth and honor—so that in your lifetime you will have no equal among kings. [14] And if

you walk in obedience to me and keep my decrees and commands as David your father did, I will give you a long life."

Not too long after he received wisdom, Solomon had his first test. An argument broke out between two women who claimed to be the biological mother of the same child. They brought the child to King Solomon's court for a verdict. Both women pleaded with the king to be given the child as they claimed to be the rightful mother. Every eye and ear of the audience focused their attention on the young king. Solomon's judgment was the beginning of the demonstration that he was the wisest king who had ever lived.

## 1 Kings 3: 24 - 28

24 Then the king said, "Bring me a sword." So they brought a sword for the king. 25 He then gave an order: "Cut the living child in two and give half to one and half to the other."
26 The woman whose son was alive was deeply moved out of love for her son and said to the king, "Please, my lord, give her the living baby! Don't kill him!" But the other said, "Neither I nor you shall have him. Cut him in two!"
27 Then the king gave his ruling: "Give the living baby to the first woman. Do not kill him; she is his mother."
28 When all Israel heard the verdict the king had given, they held the king in awe, because they saw that he had wisdom from God to administer justice.

Although we don't sit as judge like Solomon, we do make decisions and judgments that affect our lives in small and big ways. And Christians who don't pray for God's discernment end up with regret and sorrow.

Seeking God's wisdom is important for numerous reasons, but the primary reason is to avoid regret leading to grief. The Israelites experienced this with the Gibeonites. When the Gibeonites came to trick the Israelites into making a treaty with them, "The Israelites sampled their provisions but did not inquire of the LORD. Then Joshua made a treaty of peace with them to let them live, and the leaders of the assembly ratified it by oath" (Joshua 9:14-15). The Lord had commanded the Israelites to destroy their enemies completely and not to make any treaties with them. Eventually, the Gibeonites became a "thorn in the flesh" to the Jews. Avoid grief by seeking God's wisdom.

**Read one or more of these verses out loud during prayer as you seek to make wise decisions about your life. Meditate upon a particular verse throughout the day. You will gain insight about what the verse is saying. Then you will make better decisions about the situations you are facing.**

### James 3:17

17 But the wisdom that comes from heaven is first of all pure; then peace-loving, considerate, submissive, full of mercy and

good fruit, impartial and sincere.

## James 1:5

5 If any of you lacks wisdom, you should ask God, who gives generously to all without finding fault, and it will be given to you.

## Psalm 51:6

6 Yet you desired faithfulness even in the womb; you taught me wisdom in that secret place.

## Proverbs 2:6

6 For the LORD gives wisdom; from his mouth come knowledge and understanding.

## 1 Corinthians 1:24

24 but to those whom God has called, both Jews and Greeks, Christ the power of God and the wisdom of God.

## Job 12:12-13

12 Is not wisdom found among the aged? Does not long life bring understanding? 13 "To God belong wisdom and power; counsel and understanding are his.

## Proverbs 28:26

26 Those who trust in themselves are fools,

but those who walk in wisdom are kept safe.

### Proverbs 23:4

[4] Do not wear yourself out to get rich;
   do not trust your own cleverness.

### Proverbs 4:5

[5] Get wisdom, get understanding;
do not forget my words or turn away from them.

### Proverbs 16:16

[16] How much better to get wisdom than gold,
   to get insight rather than silver!

# -Chapter 17-

## Knowing God's Will through His Word

Knowing the will of God is not a matter of how good we are at guessing what God is thinking. Since He has already revealed His mind in His Word, our pursuit is understanding and obeying it. All we need to know about living an exemplary life has been written down for us. Our responsibility is to search the Scriptures to know God better and to follow Him more closely in our actions. God's Word has everything to say from how life began to how it will all end. He tells us what is wrong and what is right, and who is good and who is evil. He even tells us what we are thinking and how we should be thinking. When we submit to God's Word, God will change us.

### Hebrews 4:12

[12] For the word of God is alive and active. Sharper than any double-edged sword, it penetrates even to dividing soul and spirit, joints and marrow; it judges the thoughts and attitudes of the heart.

The Word of God is so powerful it can do what a surgeon's scalpel can't. The scalpel can only go down to the joints and marrow, but the Word of God can distinguish the soul from the spirit and separate where the motives are coming from. No one knows us like the Lord. If that isn't scary, I don't know what is. Imagine your spouse, another family member, or a friend knowing you that well. If they knew every motive you have, lying to them would be futile. And if God knows us better than we know ourselves, it stands to reason that we should follow His direction for our lives.

**Proverbs 4:20 - 22**

[20] My son, pay attention to what I say;

turn your ear to my words.

[21] Do not let them out of your sight,

keep them within your heart;

[22] for they are life to those who find them

and health to one's whole body.

The Bible is the very Word of God. If your father died before you were born and left you his will, wouldn't you want to know what he said and what he wanted you to do? If there were things in there you couldn't understand, would you not seek people who were more knowledgeable so they can explain it to you? If there was lawyer language, you would seek out a lawyer. If there was poetry, you would seek out a poet.

You would make sure you understood every word in the document. Pursue God's Word like that. Make sure you know every word. Make sure you understand every expression. Don't miss anything. Go into it with both feet and be committed to knowing His Word so you will know His will. What we know about God, including the person and work of Jesus, is found in the Bible. If the only thing you had of your dad were letters he wrote to the family, wouldn't you read them over and over? What if that was the only way you could get to know him because he was deployed as a soldier before you were born? Until he returns you would be reading those letters over and over. The word "revelation" comes from the Greek word *apokalupsis* which means "disclosure" or "unveiling." Revelation, thus, has to do with revealing, uncovering, or unveiling what previously was hidden. When used in a theological sense, "revelation" refers to God's intentional manifestation of Himself and His plans. In other words, God has revealed or unveiled His will in the Holy Bible. We can all know it by studying His Word.

## Proverbs 3:5-6

Trust in the Lord with all your heart;

do not depend on your own understanding.

Seek his will in all you do,

and he will show you which path to take. (NLT)

**Short Answers**: Knowing God's Will through His Word

**Step 1**: Read God's Word to understand God's moral law. This is God's general revelation or God's will to all mankind.

**Step 2**: If you have a question about whether something is right or wrong, look to see if the Bible addresses it. If it is not addressed, look for principles that apply to the subject such as, "Overcome evil with good" or "It is better to give than to receive."

**Step 3**: If God brings to mind a particular verse, then meditate on it day and night. God will give you insight so you will know what to do with it.

**Step 4**: Once you have interpreted and understood a passage, apply the principle and put it to action. Make an immediate plan to do what the Bible says.

# Here are some examples of how the Holy Bible reveals to us His will:

Concerning eternal life through God's Son:

## John 6:40

[40] For my Father's will is that everyone who looks to the Son and believes in him shall have eternal life, and I will raise them up at the last day."

Concerning God's plan of salvation through Jesus Christ:

## 2 Timothy 3:15

[15] and how from infancy you have known the Holy Scriptures, which are able to make you wise for salvation through faith in Christ Jesus.

## Ephesians 1:5-12

[5] he predestined us for adoption to sonship through Jesus Christ, in accordance with his pleasure and will— [6] to the praise of his glorious grace, which he has freely given us in the One he loves. [7] In him we have redemption through his blood, the forgiveness of sins, in accordance with the riches of God's grace [8] that he lavished on us. With all wisdom and understanding, [9] he made known to us the mystery of his will according to his good pleasure, which he purposed in Christ, [10]

to be put into effect when the times reach their fulfillment—to bring unity to all things in heaven and on earth under Christ. [11] In him we were also chosen, having been predestined according to the plan of him who works out everything in conformity with the purpose of his will, [12] in order that we, who were the first to put our hope in Christ, might be for the praise of his glory.

Concerning righteousness and fighting evil:

### Colossians 1:9-12

We continually ask God to fill you with the knowledge of his will through all the wisdom and understanding that the Spirit gives, [10] so that you may live a life worthy of the Lord and please him in every way: bearing fruit in every good work, growing in the knowledge of God, [11] being strengthened with all power according to his glorious might so that you may have great endurance and patience, [12] and giving joyful thanks to the Father, who has qualified you to share in the inheritance of his holy people in the kingdom of light.

### 1 Peter 2:15

[15] For it is God's will that by doing good you should silence the ignorant talk of foolish people.

**Romans 12:21**

Do not be overcome by evil, but overcome evil with good.

The Bible has much to say about salvation and righteousness because it is its primary message. But it has something to say, in some way or another, about every other subject we can think of. If a subject isn't addressed directly, it will fall under a principle that has been specifically stated. Let's say you're not clear about what kind of music you should listen to. With so many different kinds of music could the Bible have something to say about all of it? Instead of addressing all different kinds of music, we are given principles of wholesomeness. 1 Corinthians 10:23 tells us:

"I have the right to do anything," you say—but not everything is beneficial. "I have the right to do anything"—but not everything is constructive.

And Phil 4:8 also tells us:

"Finally, brothers, whatever is true, whatever is noble, whatever is right, whatever is pure, whatever is lovely, whatever is admirable—if anything is excellent or praiseworthy—think about such things."

Although we have the right or the freedom to listen to any kind of music available to us, we conscientiously make choices that are for our good, things that are praiseworthy and admirable. So many things fit into this category: food, clothing, education, sports, books, movies, hobbies, habits, jobs, and so on. God holds us responsible for the choices we make in everything. We must follow His Word and not our opinion or preferences.

## Meditate Upon God's Word

A major step toward knowing God's will through the Word is meditating upon the Word throughout the day. Unlike transcendental meditation where you empty your mind and think about nothing, meditating on God's Word is thinking about what it means. It means repeating what God said over and over and taking it apart to think about different phrases a little at a time. Let me illustrate. "In the beginning was the Word, and the Word was with God and the Word was God. He was with God in the beginning (John 1:1-2). Begin by asking yourself some questions instead of assuming things. How long ago was the beginning? Is the "beginning" of verse 1 the same as the "beginning" of the verse 2? Is it the beginning of time or was it eternity past? Is the "Word" the written word or the spoken word? How can the "Word" be God? How can the "Word" be with God? Doesn't the Word reside in God? Why does the text change from "Word" in verse 1 to "He" in verse 2? As you ask questions and think about what they mean, repeat to yourself a specific passage such as, "and the Word was God, and the Word was God, and the Word was God." Eventually, you'll realize that it's not just the Word of God, but the Word is God. God's word is Himself. God and His Word are inseparable. When we say, "A man is only as good as his word," or "Your word is your bond," or "You have my word," we are saying the same one thing: What I'm saying is true, you can count on it, and it will happen. God's Word is who He is. It is true because God doesn't lie. It will happen because He will make it happen. If the Word of God didn't exist, God wouldn't exist because the Word of God existed from the beginning because the Word was God and is God. You can see how powerful meditating on God's Word can be. Meditation on the Word is more feasible as you commit the verses to memory.

I (Joseph) have a difficult time memorizing Scripture verses, but I do better in memorizing the content and context of the biblical stories. As I read the Bible, many times a verse will impress me. What I mean by "impress" is I will realize I need to do that or I didn't know that or I needed to hear that, or I need to find out more about that etc. Christians use expressions such as "The passage spoke to me," "The passage jump out at me," "The passage was convicting," "The passage came alive," etc. to describe the same thing. These are the verses that I will write down on a small note pad and commit to memory in order to meditate on them. I will meditate on those passages word by word, line by line, and verse by verse.

As you do this, you will gain new insights that will encourage you and strengthen you in your relationship with the Lord. I was a young Christian (about a year old) when I (Jae) was meditating on God's word while brushing my teeth. As I was thinking about the words of Jesus, "The truth will set you free," the light bulb turned on. The Holy Spirit matched those words with another statement Jesus made giving me deeper insight into both. The Holy Spirit reminded me that Jesus also said, "I am the Way, the Truth, and the Life." Combining the two statements brings about a new statement: "Jesus will set you free." Since Jesus is "the Truth," we can say that. The implication of this truth is that we can't depend on some 12 step program to set us free, we can't be set free by working harder, winning the lottery, a divorce, breaking out of jail, or moving to another state or country. Only Jesus can set us free. I thought, "Wow! Thank You, Lord for opening my eyes and giving me understanding." See, whatever addictions you may have, now that you know Jesus, He will set you free. It was meditating on God's Word that brought the insight, and I was strengthened by it.

## Joshua 1:8

Keep this Book of the Law always on your lips; meditate on it day and night, so that you may be careful to do everything written in it. Then you will be prosperous and successful.

As you meditate on God's Word, study it, and then it is vital to apply it to understand God's Will through His Word. We can know God's Word inside and out, but if we as believers do not apply His Word in our daily lives, then our understanding of His will for our lives can never be fully understood. Only our actions in obedience to His Word will open the path to God's plans for our lives.

### Romans 12

[1] Therefore, I urge you, brothers and sisters, in view of God's mercy, to offer your bodies as a living sacrifice, holy and pleasing to God—this is your true and proper worship. [2] Do not conform to the pattern of this world, but be transformed by the renewing of your mind. Then you will be able to test and approve what God's will is—his good, pleasing and perfect will.

# -Chapter 18-

## Knowing God's Will through Christian Service

The local church made the announcement that they needed more volunteers, especially men for the Children's Department. The church knew that I (Joseph) had some extensive martial arts background, so they asked me if I would be interested in teaching Bible study to a small group of fourth grade boys. I knew that part of being a Christian was to serve at my local church, so I gladly accepted the offer, not knowing how difficult it would be. All the teachers in the Elementary Department were so thrilled that I came on board to serve, but I joined in on the celebration not realizing the reason for the festivities.

On the first day of class, I realized why the teachers were so joyful about my serving. They had brought in all the fourth grade trouble makers to my class, hoping that I would straighten them out, in the Word of course. The commitment I made was to serve for a year, and the boys were not too thrilled to have me as their teacher. However, by the end of the year the boys had developed a great sense of respect for me, each other, the Bible, but most importantly their identity in Jesus Christ. The class went so well, and I as a teacher learned so much more about the Bible that I signed up for an additional year. But I wasn't sure if the boys were as excited about my return as I was.

**Short Answers**: Knowing God's Will through Christian Service.

**Step 1**: Serve the Local Church using your talent and spiritual gifts. Try things out if you don't know your spiritual gifts.

**Step 2**: Serve by giving financially from your heart and start with tithing.

**Step 3**: Share the gospel wherever you go. Ask the Lord for opportunities to share.

It was during this period of serving that I started to wonder if God had a plan for me to be in full or part-time ministry. The more I served and the more I studied about serving, the more I became interested in shepherding and leading His church. Eventually I prayed to God, "What I can do for You?" The conviction for me to attend seminary became so strong that I applied. While attending seminary, I became the Youth

Pastor of the same church where I had served as the boys' Bible study teacher. Later I also served as the Young Adults Pastor. By serving at the local church, I was able to seek God's will for my life and sense His leading.

## Serving the Local Church

What does the Bible say about serving? Through service the body of believers will glorify God by building up and encouraging one another and reaching unbelievers. God commands us to serve, that "Each of you should use whatever gift you have received to serve others, as faithful stewards of God's grace in its various forms" (1 Peter 4:10), and this is one of the ways we worship God (1 Peter 4:11, Romans 12:1). When each of us do our part in using our God-given gifts to serve others, we are helping to build up both the local church and the universal church-made up of all believers throughout the world: "...to equip his people for works of service, so that the body of Christ may be built up..." (Eph. 4:12).

And we serve the body because we love it. The members of the body are our siblings in Christ. Jesus himself loved the local church:

### Ephesians 5:25
25 Husbands, love your wives, just as Christ loved the church
and gave himself up for her

This is why it is so important to continue to meet with fellow believers and spend time with them. If we love each other, we should be spending time together to have godly fun and build each other up:

### Hebrews 10:24-25

24 And let us consider how we may spur one another on toward love and good deeds, 25 not giving up meeting together, as some are in the habit of doing, but encouraging one another—and all the more as you see the Day approaching.

## "And let us consider":

1. God wants his children to be thinking about one another, fellowshipping, and praying for one another.
2. God does not want His children to be in isolation, but to be together as a family.
3. God tells us to spend time together and consider one another's needs and how we might be able to best minister and serve each other.
4. God tells us to look for ways to "spur," "stir up," or "incite" one another toward "love and good deeds."
5. God says we should not give up meeting together in public worship, Bible studies, fellowship, and prayer meetings.
6. Even more so "as you see the Day approaching," which is the day the Lord returns for His children.

As a matter of fact if you are not involved in your local church, you are out of fellowship with the Lord. It's like saying I love you dad, but I don't want to take care of my siblings? How can that be acceptable to Him?

## Serving with Your Talents and Gifts

Encouraging and praying for one another is necessary. It's part of fellowship, but that is not all we do as believers. We are called to serve. That means we clean the sanctuary, hand out the bulletins, write for the newsletter, contact the missionaries, prepare snacks for fellowship, sing in the choir, welcome the visitors, serve as deacons, lead the Sunday school class, change the oil of the church van, visit the sick, visit the elderly, cook for mothers who just gave birth, babysit for couples with children, play in the band, monitor the sound system, lead activities, plan picnics, plan retreats, plan surprises, build props for Christmas plays, build storage shelves, lend someone your car, give one of your vehicles to someone in need, collect some money and send your pastor on a vacation, help with parking, translate the sermon, fix the plumbing, fix the computer, fix the copy machine, decorate the classrooms, teach the church how to invest, how to lose weight, how to eat well, how to evangelize, and how to garden, and much, much more. These are just a "few" ways to serve the body. Whatever abilities you have, use them to serve the church. Look at it this way. If you are a member of a family and don't do any chores, how are you helping the family thrive? If the parents are the only ones who are "serving" the family, how will the rest feel like they are contributing? Not serving will only breed selfishness. On the other hand if you took on a summer job for your brother so he could go on a mission trip, you will be blessed because you gave to God's cause, and your sibling would be blessed because you sacrificed your time and money to help him go.

But in order to maximize your effectiveness in serving, you must focus on serving in the areas of your talents and spiritual gifts. There are similarities and differences between talents and spiritual gifts, both are given by our heavenly Father and are intended to be used to benefit others. 1 Corinthians 12:7 says, "Now to each one the manifestation of the Spirit is given for the common good."

People in general, regardless of their belief in God will have a talent. My wife has a talent in singing, and she can sing like an angel where as I (Joseph) have to practice in order to sing well and even then my kids will be ask me to stop singing out loud (they can be too honest sometimes). Natural talents can vary from sports, music, art, academics, and creativity. In the same way Spiritual gifts are given to all believers by the Holy Spirit. Every believer will have at least one. Romans 12:6 says, "We have different gifts, according to the grace given to each of us. If your gift is prophesying, then prophesy in accordance with your faith." Anything involving Spiritual gifts "are the work of one and the same Spirit, and he distributes them to each one, just as he determines" (1 Corinthians 12:11). The Holy Spirit gives to the new believer the spiritual gift(s) He desires the believer to have. Spiritual gifts include but are not limited to prophesying, pastoring, teaching, evangelism, wisdom, knowledge, faith, healing, miracles, spiritual discernment, languages, interpretation of languages, encouraging, giving, and showing mercy (1 Corinthians 12:8-11; Romans 12:6-8). All Christians are to serve the body using their gifts. In doing so, you will find fulfillment and encouragement in advancing God's kingdom. In order to understand better spiritual gifts, please consult with your local church leaders.

## Understanding Your Calling

### Called to Faith

Not everyone is "called" to be a full-time minister, but everyone is "called" to the faith. Every believer has experienced a call to faith when the challenge came to trust in Jesus Christ through trials and tribulations. From every walk of life we were called to join His kingdom. The Bible is clear; God calls all to receive salvation and redemption that can only be found through Jesus Christ. 1 Corinthians 1:9 tell us, "God is faithful, who has called you into fellowship with his Son, Jesus Christ our Lord."

## 1 Timothy 6:12

¹² Fight the good fight of the faith. Take hold of the eternal life to which you were called when you made your good confession in the presence of many witnesses.

## Called to Minister

After we join His family, God gives us some duties. We are called to serve one another or to minister to one another. Every believer is called to minister to other believers using our God given natural talent and special anointed gifts. As a child of God we play a significant role in God's work and represent Jesus Christ as ambassadors.

## 2 Corinthians 5:20

²⁰ We are therefore Christ's ambassadors, as though God were making his appeal through us.

However, there is a big difference between a "Call to Minister" and a "Call into the Ministry."

## Called into the Ministry

Throughout the Bible God called or chose certain people for specific purposes. A call "into" ministry is God's invitation to be set apart for the purpose of primarily serving His people. Paul was called to be an "apostle," "preacher," and "teacher" of the Gentiles and while in prison he noted, "I press on toward the goal to win the prize for which God has called me hea-venward in Christ Jesus" (Philippians 3:14). If you think you have been "Called into the Ministry," dedicate yourself to prayer, find Scriptural support, get confirmation from wise counsel, and make sure your spouse agrees with you. At first try to refuse. If you are really called, God will convince you even if you try to run.

For every move toward ministry, I made sure that my wife was in agreement with me. When God first convicted me to attend seminary, I asked my wife for her opinion and prayer support. At first, my wife disagreed with me about attending seminary, so I waited for God to move her heart. A week later, the Lord moved my wife's heart to allow me to start seminary. When churches asked me to serve in their ministry, I made sure that my wife was in agreement with me to serve those ministries. If you are married, get the full support of your wife, for without it the ministry will be divided, your prayers will be hindered, and you will lose endurance. If you are truly called by God, He will make a way for you to enter into minis-try by all the right means. He won't take any shortcuts to get you there.

### Ephesians 4:11-12

[11] So Christ himself gave the apostles, the prophets, the evan-gelists, the pastors and teachers, [12] to equip his people for works of service, so that the body of Christ may be built up

# Serving through Giving Financially

It took ten years to build the business but only a day to collapse it because of one employee with a gambling addiction. I (Joseph) lost everything, including my clients, assets, and business property worth thousands. Losing the business was one thing but losing my house and not knowing where I was going to get enough money to feed our three children took its toll. It was during this very difficult period of my life that I learned the most important lesson about giving to God.

My wife and I knew of a small church that was in need of finances to run their Children's Ministry. What was attention-grabbing was that God chose this period of our lives to prompt us to give all that we had to this church. It wasn't much, but it would have helped us last a little long before going totally broke. I fought with God, "God! Are you crazy? Where am I going to get the money to help this church when our family is in so much need?" God knew we had just a few hundred bucks for groceries, so I pleaded with Him to let me keep it, but His conviction was too strong. It sounded as if His words were audible, "Do you trust me with ALL your heart? You know that I will never leave you nor forsake you, I love your kids more than you, and surely I will provide for your family." Both my wife and I were convicted in our hearts to give. We gave the church the money knowing that God would truly provide for our family.

We have seen God work His amazing miracles before, so we trusted God and obeyed. In less than a week, there was a knock on our door, and the postman asked us to sign for the certified mail. We opened it, and it was a check with no name but the amount was double of what we gave. For over two years we struggled financially, but He constantly reminded us that all things on earth and in heaven belong to Him. God not only provided for our basic necessities, but He also drew our family closer together and closer to Himself. "And my God will supply every need of yours according to his riches in glory in Christ Jesus" (Philippians 4:19).

Our children were also learning the importance of giving from their hearts. When our children are given money from friends and family, they know that 10 percent goes directly to God, 10 percent to those in need (charity, missions, etc.), 10 percent into savings, and the remaining amount for however they choose to use it. One time, our oldest daughter received a considerable amount of money as a gift. She deducted the usual amount and with the remaining amount in hand went shopping with her mother. As they went to the store, she felt convicted not to spend the remaining amount on a toy she had been wanting for a long time. She decided to save the money and use it more wisely.

**1 Timothy 6:18**

¹⁸ Command them to do good, to be rich in good deeds, and to be generous and willing to share.

## Giving from the Heart

From the Old Testament we understand the importance of tithing, which means giving to God ten percent of the best we have. This is the gross amount and not the net. The tithe is a reflection of our gratitude for His provision as we read in Leviticus 27:30, "A tithe of everything from the land, whether grain from the soil or fruit from the trees, belongs to the LORD; it is holy to the LORD."

In the Old Testament, tithing was mandatory and failing to tithe was described as robbing God. Malachi 3:8 says, "Will a mere mortal rob God? Yet you rob me. 'But you ask, 'How are we robbing you?' 'In tithes and offerings.'" However, it is important to understand that we no longer live under the Old Testament law, but under a new law. *The New Testament helps us to evaluate our giving not by how much we give, but how we give.* It is our heart attitude in giving that God judges.

In the gospel of Mark, we see Jesus watching the crowd of people put their money into the temple treasury. Many rich people threw in large amounts, but the poor widow came and put in two very small copper coins, worth only a fraction of a penny. Jesus was moved by the heart of this widow.

### Mark 12:43-44

[43] Calling his disciples to him, Jesus said, "Truly I tell you, this poor widow has put more into the treasury than all the others. [44] They all gave out of their wealth; but she, out of her poverty, put in everything—all she had to live on."

In God's eyes, the value of the offering is not determined by the amount. Jesus tells us that the wealthy gave large amounts, but the widow's offering was of much greater value because she gave "all" that she had. It was a costly sacrifice, and more importantly it was by faith.

The Scriptures tell us in Mark 12:41 that Jesus "sat down opposite the place where the offerings were put and watched the crowd putting their money into the temple treasury." Our Father in heaven is "watching" and observing how we give today. If we give with a stingy or stubborn heart, to be seen by men, then our Father will have to use measures to change us. How can we be like He is if we are not generous? The widow must have struggled very deeply about what would happen to her without any money, but her faith in God to provide was even stronger. Seeing that, do you think the Lord didn't drop abundant provisions on her lap? If your son gave his entire savings to support the relief efforts in Haiti after the earthquake of 2010, would you be reluctant to buy him his necessities? You would be so proud you'd buy him twice the number of gifts he received last Christmas. Sometimes you just have to test God to see if He is true to His word concerning the tithe.

### Malachi 3:10-12

[10] Bring the whole tithe into the storehouse, that there may be food in my house. Test me in this," says the LORD Almighty, "and see if I will not throw open the floodgates of heaven and pour out so much blessing that there will not be room enough to store it. [11] I will prevent pests from devouring your crops, and the vines in your fields will not drop their fruit before it is ripe," says the LORD Almighty. [12] "Then all the nations will call you blessed, for yours will be a delightful land," says the LORD Almighty.

The quickest way to test a believer's faith in the Lord is to challenge him to give. How he gives and how much he gives will indicate what he thinks of God. It will reveal his mindset of where everything comes from. If everything comes from God, He should be the one to one tell us what to do with it. Think of it this way: When He gives you $1000, He's really giving you $900 because $100 belongs to Him. If you feel sore about giving up $100, remember He could have given you nothing, then, you won't have anything to tithe. Which do you prefer? Do you have faith that He will provide? Do you think the one who provided for our eternal relationship with Him will skimp on our daily needs?

### James 2:26

[26]For as the body apart from the spirit is dead, so also faith apart from works is dead.

**Recommendations for Giving**: Begin by offering God ten percent of your gross income. If you have to downsize your lifestyle to tithe, do it because that means you were living above the means God has provided. It would be irresponsible to live above our income and make the excuse we can't tithe because of it.

### Proverbs 3:9-10

[9] Honor the LORD with your wealth,
with the firstfruits of all your crops;
[10] then your barns will be filled to overflowing,
and your vats will brim over with new wine.

If your income changes from month to month, then do your best to calculate each month's gross divided by the number of Sunday services in that month. Pre-give if you're going on vacation. Don't have the mentality that since you weren't at church a certain week, you are not responsible for that week's tithe. At the end of the year check to see if you've covered at least the tithe and make up the difference if you haven't. Chances are you've had additional sources of income that you didn't account for. If married and both are working, make sure you sum both incomes in order to calculate the tithe. When you give faithfully and regularly, God will honor and bless your commitment. "Commit to the LORD whatever you do, and he will establish your plans" (Proverbs 16:3).

### Exodus 23:25

[25] Worship the LORD your God, and his blessing will be on your food and water. I will take away sickness from among you,

## Sharing the Gospel: The Call to Duty

"Evangelism" (see appendix) is defined as the practice of spreading the Christian gospel in order to fulfill the Great Commission (Matthew 28:19-20). In other words, evangelism is simply the Christian duty of sharing the gospel with those who don't know it.

### Matthew 28:19-20

[19] Therefore go and make disciples of all nations, baptizing them in the name of the Father and of the Son and of the Holy Spirit, [20] and teaching them to obey everything I have com-

manded you. And surely I am with you always, to the very end of the age."

This central command is known as the "Great Commission" and NOT the "Great Suggestion." This is Jesus' last command in the book of Matthew so it holds great significance to all who call themselves followers of Christ. Many understand Acts 1:8 as part of the Great Commission as well, "But you will receive power when the Holy Spirit comes on you; and you will be my witnesses in Jerusalem, and in all Judea and Samaria, and to the ends of the earth." The combined understanding of Matthew 28:19-20 and Acts 1:8 is that the Great Commission is accomplished by the power of the Holy Spirit. We are to be Christ's witnesses, fulfilling the Great Commission in our cities (Jerusalem), in our states and countries (Judea and Samaria), and anywhere else God sends us (to the ends of the earth).

In order to fulfill the Great Commission the local church must "equip his *(God's)* people for works of service, so that the body of Christ may be built up" (Ephesians 4:12). Evangelism is a duty of all Christians, and we are required to go out into the sinful world to spread God's Word. Evangelism is also a privilege. God has commissioned us to represent Him and speak on His behalf.

Your home church should offer training and resources to help you understand how to reach unbelievers. Consult with your church leaders and ask for accountability and prayer support. Without prayer your message will fall on deaf ears because Satan will make their hearts rock hard. Prepare your heart also. You are not responsible for the conversion of those who don't know Jesus. You are responsible to be faithful and obedient to God's command. He will do the rest.

Consult with your church leaders to get equipped for evangelism; however, if your church does not have any evangelism programs, training, or teaching materials, below is a simple principle that can assist you in sharing your faith.

## P.A.L. Principle
### P: Prayer

**Step 1:** Prayer is to the foundation for sharing the message of Jesus. We are waging a spiritual war (Ephesians 6:12). There are 4 parts to evangelism prayer.

**First**: Pray for the people who will hear the message and that their hearts will be open to receive the gospel. Make sure to mention to God the person's name.

**Second**: Ask God to provide the time or opportunity to share the gospel or your own testimony.

**Third**: Ask God to open the other person's heart to receive the message of salvation.

**Fourth:** Ask the Lord for wisdom, discernment, and courage to speak the truth in love.

## A: Apply God's Love

**Step 2:** As you meet with the person you were praying about, speak in love. Don't argue, but urge. Jesus tells us that the second greatest commandment is to "Love your neighbor as yourself" (Matthew 22:39). If you are not sure what to say, ask the Holy Spirit to guide you in your weakness. Romans 8:26 says, "In the same way, the Spirit helps us in our weakness. We do not know what we ought to pray for, but the Spirit himself intercedes for us through wordless groans."

There are many times when I (Joseph) prayed this while listening to the other person. I simply say in my mind, "Holy Spirit, guide me in my words, I'm not exactly sure what to say." Other times, I'll pray, "Lord, do you want me to 'plant' or 'water' today?" To "plant" or "water" comes from 1 Corinthians 3:7, where Paul the author tells us that "neither the one who plants nor the one who waters is anything, but only God, who makes things grow." Listen for God. He will guide you.

## L: Leave the outcome to God

**Step 3:** If you are afraid to share the gospel for fear of rejection, you are not alone. If you live by fear, you are defeated even before you approach the person. The reason we pray is because we can't work on the person's heart. The Holy Spirit opens the heart of the other person to hear the message. Even after trying all these if the person still rejects your message, realize that the person is not rejecting you but God.

It is the Holy Spirit's job to convict and convert the unbeliever unto salvation in Jesus Christ. It is God alone who can draw them to Himself (John 6:44) and God alone who enables them to come to Him (John 6:65). Remember, God did not ask you to win someone to Christ; He just called you to be faithful and obedient. Therefore, make sure you leave the results to God and focus on being obedient to His commands.

### 2 Peter 3:9

9 The Lord is not slow in keeping his promise, as some understand slowness. Instead he is patient with you, not wanting anyone to perish, but everyone to come to repentance.

# -Chapter 19-

## Wise Counsel and God's Timing

### Seeking Wise Counsel

Seek wise counsel from mature Christians before making a big decision-something that has lasting consequences such as buying a house, relocating for a job, getting married, starting a business, deciding the type of education for your child, etc. My friend's father was about to have heart surgery, but during prayer, he was prompted by the Holy Spirit to get a second opinion. Praise the Lord. The wise counsel from another specialist saved his father from major surgery. All he needed was some heart medication, a proper diet, and regular exercise. He recovered fully in three months without the unnecessary surgery.

### Proverbs 22:17-21

[17] Pay attention and turn your ear to the sayings of the wise;
apply your heart to what I teach,
[18] for it is pleasing when you keep them in your heart
and have all of them ready on your lips.
[19] So that your trust may be in the LORD,
I teach you today, even you.
[20] Have I not written thirty sayings for you,

sayings of counsel and knowledge,
21 teaching you to be honest and to speak the truth,
so that you bring back truthful reports
to those you serve?

**Short Answers**: Knowing God's Will through wise counsel and God's timing

**Step 1**: Wait patiently, pray, stay in the Word and the Lord will give you confirmation, conviction, and peace in your heart.

**Step 2**: Seek wise counsel from mature Christians before making big decisions. God may speak through them and give you a message of wisdom and discernment.

**Step 3**: Once you have received the counsel, make sure to always give any advice from people back to God and allow Him to confirm the advice, deny it, show another way, or wait upon it.

Getting married is a life changing event, and yet many Christians never seek the advice of mature Christians, wise friends, family members, or Christian premarital counselors to confirm if their potential mate is right for them. Some people who are divorced say they knew that something was not right from the beginning, but ignored the warnings from friends and family members. Once the wedding took place, it was too late to turn back. Now anger, bitterness, and emotional trauma are all that remain. In most situations, much of this could have been avoided with proper counsel. See if this scenario is familiar.

Joan is excited about Tony, a man she met recently, and begins the relationship in earnest. She is so emotionally charged that she sees nothing but sunshine and clear skies. Once in a while she sees something that could be a problem, but her optimistic outlook quickly returns her to the land of bliss. When her family and friends meet Tony, they express their concerns and warn her to take more time evaluating his potential. They advise her to get some premarital counseling. Some strongly urge Joan to break off the relationship. She disagreed. There was no earthly way she was going to let this one go. She knows what she's doing. She's old enough to make her own decision. A grand wedding ceremony, an elaborate reception, and a son later, she was divorced in a matter of 2 years. You may know people like that, maybe even several. But it doesn't have to happen that way.

Consider the alternative: A young man named Jake meets Linda, and even though they've gotten to know each other only a short time, she propositions him by stripping in front of him. He nobly helps her dress and sends her home and doesn't see her again. Later, Jake was ready to pursue the woman of his dreams and in God's timing he met Donna. She was Asian and her father disapproved of the relationship because he was white. When He sought counsel, Jake was advised to honor her father and pray that the Lord would change her father's mind. Eventually, God did and they were blessed to be married. Two children later and happily married, they have the blessing of God follow them wherever they go.

## Proverbs 1:5

⁵Let the wise hear and increase in learning,
and the one who understands obtain guidance,

## Proverbs 11:14

¹⁴Where there is no guidance, a people falls,
but in an abundance of counselors there is safety.

The Proverbs are very clear. Guidance from mature and wise counselors will bring safety, clarity, and confirmation of God's will. During prayer you will most likely be given a prompting or conviction from the Holy Spirit. This will be followed by supporting text from the Scriptures. The Holy Spirit never contradicts the Bible and the Scriptures will never contradict God. Once the leading of the Holy Spirit match the Scriptures, seek wise counsel from a mentor, a mature Christian friend, a pastor, or a professional in the field to confirm the Lord's leading.

I (Joseph) had a personal situation in which I needed to make an important decision. This was a turning point in my life, and wanting to make the right decision I approached a pastor friend who was in a meeting with a well-respected Christian leader in the community. Both leaders were open to hearing the situation and agreed to pray together before giving their counsel. Surprisingly, each gave a different response. Walking out confused, I gave their advice to God and the Holy Spirit gave me peace concerning the input of one of the leaders. This is when I learned to always give any advice from people back to God and allow Him to either confirm the advice, deny it, show another way, or wait upon it.

Wise counselors will help you better understand the issues to consider, and during those times when you may not even be aware of the issues to weigh, the counselors may share a perspective out of the ordinary. The goal in seeking wise counsel is to cover all the bases so you can make decisions with knowledge instead of ignorance. Ultimately, God is the supreme counselor in guiding and directing your path, and you are solely responsible for the decisions you make. Make them to the glory of God by seeking wise counsel. Eventually, through the wise counsel from one of the leaders mentioned above, the Lord led me into full-time ministry.

**John 14:26**

²⁶But the Helper, the Holy Spirit, whom the Father will send in my name, he will teach you all things and bring to your remembrance all that I have said to you.

## Waiting Patiently for God's Timing

By waiting patiently in prayer the Lord will give you confirmation, conviction, and peace in your heart when it is time to move forward. Patience has got to be my (Joseph) weakest virtue. I have always been a goal setter, time maker, and visionary, so waiting upon a decision or confirmation from God has got to be one of the most difficult processes I have to endure. Nevertheless, patiently waiting through prayer has taught me a new meaning of the expression "successful timing."

Sometimes, when seeking God's will, you might feel God is not hearing your prayers even when you have applied all the methods mentioned in this book. David was a young man around 15 years of age when he was anointed to be the next king after Saul. However, David did not become king until the age of thirty. During this long period of waiting, God was training David to be the next ruler. The 15 years of waiting was actually, 15 years of preparation for responsibility that he would receive. 1 Chronicles 12:23-40 describes the great assembly that gathered in Hebron to recognize David as king over all Israel. Chronicles describes the impressive army that came to Hebron, over 340,000 men. It then describes the scene:

### 1 Chronicles 12:38-40

38 All these were fighting men who volunteered to serve in the ranks. They came to Hebron fully determined to make David king over all Israel. All the rest of the Israelites were also of one mind to make David king. 39 The men spent three days there with David, eating and drinking, for their families had supplied provisions for them. 40 Also, their neighbors from as far away as Issachar, Zebulun and Naphtali came bringing food on donkeys, camels, mules and oxen. There were plentiful supplies of flour, fig cakes, raisin cakes, wine, olive oil, cattle and sheep, for there was joy in Israel.

With God, delay has a purpose and we must trust that He knows what He's doing and wait patiently for our turn.

We read in Genesis 12:2-3, Abram was 75 years old when God promised to make him into a "great nation." God even changed Abram's name to Abraham, "for I have made you a father of many nations" (Genesis 17:5). But there were two strikes against him, his wife was beyond child-bearing age and she was barren. Even though naturally, what God had promised was impossible; supernaturally, the promise of God was fulfilled with the birth of Isaac after 25 years. Why the long wait? And how will we know the time is right for our decisions?

I have three children, and each child has expressed the desire to mature. But without proper emotional, social, physical, and psychological training, my children will only grow in stature. Being tall and childish is an awkward combination. Soldiers have to go through the rigors of boot camp, learn how to use weapons, and practice combat tactics before being deployed for war. Without the training, proper gear, and weapons, the soldiers will suffer defeat. To use a martial arts analogy, you cannot jump from a white belt to a black belt over night. There are several belts that must be earned before the student receives the test for his black belt.

As a former martial arts instructor, I've had many anxious white belts ask me when the next belt promotion will be. But unless an instructor asks a student to prepare for the next test, the student was to be faithfully training in their present belt. If the anxious student continues to ask, the student will continue to receive the same answer, to wait until they are fully prepared. Sometimes frequently asking for God's will is a preoccupational distraction for the believer. Instead, focus on maturing and growing in the character of Christ. When it is time, God will give you the assignment He has prepared.

# How and when will I know God's calling for my life?

Know that as you mature, you will have greater discernment of God's will then you have now. You will express greater trust in His ability to lead you. You will have more confidence in Him to provide the necessary guidance to get you to your destination. You will fret less and focus more. Instead of asking for His will you don't know, you will be doing His will you do know.

Many years ago, I (Joseph) was very passionate about reaching young adults for Christ, so I started a ministry called New Generation or NGen for short. Although righteously conceived, it ended up failing because it was not the right time for it. Did I jump the gun or was God giving me some ministry experience? If He was leading me, then God was giving me understanding of ministry timing. If it was selfish ambition, God was showing me the consequence of running ahead of Him. Unfortunately, it was the latter because I wanted to build His kingdom. It wasn't that God was calling me to start this ministry. I thought it was a good idea based on the need. Credit is a great way to judge calling. Who will receive the credit when all is said and done? If you get the credit, then it won't be His calling or timing. But if He gets the credit, you can be almost certain that it was the Lord's calling and timing.

I (Jae) was contemplating attending seminary, partly because of the sensing in my spirit and partly by the encouragement of my pastor and close Christian friends. Over a period of six months I prayed about the calling to receive confirmation from the Lord. Once I was convinced that I was called, I sought additional confirmation by consulting my pastor and other leaders. In a conversation with one of those leaders, we discussed the possibility of deferring my admission for a year in order to save money for the education. This chat occurred in the car while returning from a leadership retreat. When I arrived home, my sister called me to the den in order to make a proposition in my favor. She handed me a check and told me that I didn't have to contribute to the family finances any more since I would need the money for seminary. The three hundred dollars I received was a token from God to testify He was sending me this year. As I thought about it, it made sense. If I had saved up money for a year, I would have been somewhat comfortable knowing that I had what I needed. I would have given credit to myself for taking charge and providing for my needs. On the other hand, if I don't have the savings and go now, I have to rely on the Lord and He would get the credit for providing everything I needed. I understood and prepared to go that year. As predicted, I had to rely on the Lord for all the provisions. And better than I could have predicted, He provided all that I needed. All the credit went to Him, and the calling and timing was confirmed.

# Then, how will I know God's timing?

Continue to:

1. Pray daily
2. Read the Word on a regular basis
3. Serve the local church using your: Talent, Spiritual Gifts and Treasures
4. Share the gospel
5. Seek wise counsel but give it back to God for the final decision
6. Wait for God's timing
7. God will open doors

God's agenda is that through every aspect of our Christian lives, we get to know Him better. He will use all of life to draw us closer to Himself. At each stage of our maturity, He will have assignments for us to accomplish. Be eager to fulfill His calling, but be even more eager to know your heavenly Father better. May the Lord richly work in your life as you walk with Him.

## Isaiah 55:8-11

[8]"For my thoughts are not your thoughts, neither are your ways my ways," declares the LORD. [9]"As the heavens are higher than the earth, so are my ways higher than your ways and my thoughts than your thoughts. [10]As the rain and the

snow come down from heaven, and do not return to it without watering the earth and making it bud and flourish, so that it yields seed for the sewer and bread for the eater, [11]so is my word that goes out from my mouth: It will not return to me empty, but will accomplish what I desire and achieve the purpose for which I sent it.

# Appendix A

# Basic Christian Terms

**Old Testament** (OT): **OT** *Bible* is the first of the two main divisions of the Christian Bible. The 39 books of the OT records the history of the Jewish people, God's chosen race. In Jewish tradition, it is divided into three parts: the Law (Torah or the Pentateuch), the Prophets, and the Writings.

**New Testament** (NT): **NT** *Bible* is the second part of the two main divisions of the Christian Bible. The 27 books of the NT are a collection of writings consisting of the Gospels, Acts of the Apostles, Pauline and other Epistles, and the book of Revelation, composed soon after Christ's death and added to the Jewish writings of the Old Testament to make up the Christian Bible.

**Messiah:** In the Old Testament the Messiah is the promised and expected deliverer of the Jewish people as the "anointed one" or Christ-the Savior. Jesus is the promised one, the anticipated redeemer of the Jews, who was sent by God to free his people and who delivered mankind from their sins. The Jewish people believe that the Messiah or Christ has not yet come.

**Yahweh:** This name comes from the Old Testament as transliterated from the Hebrew consonants YHVH. Yahweh is the personal name of God in the Hebrew Bible, and it means "I am."

**Jehovah:** Another personal name of God in the Hebrew Scriptures, Jehovah has a dubious origin. The Jews never pronounced the name of God for fear of mispronouncing it and therefore dishonoring Him or taking His name in vain. Instead, they used Adonai or Lord. Unaware of this, the translators put the consonant of YHVH with vowels of Adonai and came up with a hybrid Jehovah. It's actually a misnomer.

**Immanuel:** This literally means, "God with us." Before Jesus was born, an angel appeared to Joseph in a dream and said that Jesus would be named Immanuel (Matthew 1:23).

**Trinity:** Also called "Holy Trinity" which is a Christian doctrine that states that there is one God in three equal divine persons: God the Father, Son as Jesus and the Holy Spirit. This word is not found in Scripture, but used to express the doctrine of the unity of God as subsisting in three equal (value but not in rank) distinct Persons.

**Apostle:** An Apostle or "Messenger" is one of the early 12 disciples of Jesus who carried the Christian message (preached the gospel) into the world. The word "Apostle" can also refer to the first or the best-known Christian missionary in any region or country such as the apostle Paul. It is the highest of the five offices or titles in the New Testament, the other four are prophet, teacher, evangelist, and pastor.

**Christian:** A person that is a follower or disciple of Jesus Christ and who believes Jesus to be God.

**Born Again:** This term was coined by the Lord as recorded in John 3:3. It refers to a person becoming a God of child by the power of the Holy Spirit. This second birth (or rebirth) is a spiritual one. Nobody becomes a Christian without being born again.

**Evangelical Christian:** Related to or being a Christian, emphasizing personal salvation solely through being born again with a commitment to Jesus Christ and believes that the four Gospels of the Bible have no errors.

**Sin:** The simple definition of sin is anything that is contrary to the character of God. "Be holy because I am holy," is what He said. Anything outside of that is sin. Whether it is a sin of commission or omission, if it is outside the character of God, we have sinned.

**Repentance:** Repentance begins with a sense of conviction of sin and results in the turning away from it. A truly repentant person desires to live a holy life.

**Revival:** Spiritual renewal, reawakening of faith, or God's quickening visitation of the body of believers initiated by the Holy Spirit. It can also refer to an evangelistic meeting or service intended to affect such a reawakening to those present which results in a deeper religious experience, mass conversions, and a greater fervor for holy living and evangelism.

**Evangelism:** The practice of spreading the Christian gospel in order to fulfill the Great Commission in the Bible (Matthew 28:19-20).

**Denomination:** A religious group having a distinctive interpretation of a religious faith, common beliefs or principles and usually its own organization and local congregations, subscribing to common creed and acknowledging the authority of a common body or head.

**Presbyterian:** Relating to, or designating Church government by presbyters or lay elders or its system of government by presbyters.

**Lutheran:** A follower of Martin Luther (1483 – 1546), who is the German initiator of the Reformation, or a member of a Lutheran Church relating to Luther or his doctrines, the most important being justification by faith alone, consubstantiation, and the authority of the Bible.

**Methodist:** A member of any of the Nonconformist denominations that derive from the system of faith and practice initiated by John Wesley and his followers as an effective "method" for leading Christians toward the scriptural goal of holiness.

**Baptist:** A Christian denomination that affirm the necessity of the believer's baptism or the immersion of adults in water upon a personal profession of Christian faith.

**Pentecostal:** Relating to any of various Christian groups that emphasize the charismatic aspects or "sign gifts" of Christianity and adopt a fundamental attitude to the Bible.

**Assemblies of God:** The largest American Pentecostal denomination formed in 1914 by various Pentecostal churches and marked by faith healing and speaking in tongues.

**Bishop:** Higher order of ministers or clergyman having spiritual and administrative powers over a diocese or province. Bishops can also be the chief pastors of the church in most Christian traditions and are consecrated to rule a particular diocese or part of a church within an ecclesiastical (church) province.

**Reverend:** Used as a title of respect in addressing clergymen or prefixed to the name of a member of the clergy or a religious order.

**Pastor:** Title of minister, priest or clergyman in charge of a local church and who exercises spiritual guidance over a congregation.

**Priest:** An ordained person to act as a mediator between God and man in administering the sacraments, certain rites, preaching, blessing, guiding, and other religious ritual obligations.

**Rabbi:** The chief religious official of a synagogue, trained usually in a theological seminary and duly ordained, who delivers the sermon at a religious service and performs ritualistic, pastoral, educational, and other functions in and related to his or her capacity as a spiritual leader of Judaism and the Jewish community.

**Sacraments:** A religious ceremony or rite using material means and verbal formulae by which believers partake in, commemorate, or respond to the mystery of Christ and through which he communicates and relates to his body of believers.

**Apocalypse:** Another name for the last book in the New Testament, The Book of Revelation. The Greek word for apocalypse is "revelation" or "unveiling" which reveals things normally hidden and unveils the future or deals with the end of the present world order and the coming of a new kingdom.

**Rapture:** The "caught up or rapture" theology is the experience and anticipation of believers meeting Jesus Christ midway in the air upon his return to earth based on 1 Thessalonians 4:14-17.

**Millennium:** A period of a thousand years during which Christ will reign with his people over the earth based on Revelation 20:1-7. This is considered to be a time of peace, happiness and general righteousness.

**Bible Concordance:** An index of names, words, and phrases, showing their book, chapter, and verse in the Bible.

**Bible Commentary:** A series of comments, explanations, or explanatory essays on the Holy Scriptures which serves to illustrate a point and help readers understand it.

**Exegesis**: (from the Greek 'to lead out') is a critical explanation or interpretation of the Bible. The word is used to describe an approach to interpreting a passage in the Scriptures by critical analysis where the meaning of the text is derived from terms, structure, and context.

**Inerrancy**: The Bible is free from error in all it affirms in the original text.

**Infallibility**: The Bible is unfailing in its purpose and could not have factual errors. In another words the Bible is incapable of failure or error.

**Sufficiency**: The Bible contains all needed information for Christian living.

**Authority**: The Bible carries the right to prescribe beliefs and actions.

# Appendix B

---

## **Commitment**

I (Print Name) _____ will make a

_____ (length of term) commitment to read the Bi-

ble each day from day_____ to day_____

I pledge to give (Time length: 15 minutes to one hour) _____

in the (day or evening) _____ starting from

(month) _____ day _____ year _____

Sign Name: _____

Date: _____

Witness Name: _____

Date: _____

---

Cut this page and keep in your Bible

**JnJ Publishing**
Real, Practical and Super-natural; Ministry Resources
for the Next Generation

For Questions or Comments: www.JnJpublishing.com

<u>Coming Soon:</u>

**Hiring an**
**English Ministry Pastor**
*& Beyond*
In an Asian American Church context

찾는 방법

우리 교회에 필요한 영어권 사역 목화자는?

Made in the USA
Middletown, DE
12 August 2018